I0155995

Sir John Fortescue's Banners Forward!

Sir John Fortescue's Banners Forward!

The Development & Campaigns
of British Armies 1066–1642

J. W. Fortescue

LEONAUR

Sir John Fortescue's Banners Forward!
The Development & Campaigns of British Armies 1066-1642
by J. W. Fortescue

FIRST EDITION

Text taken from *A History of the British Army*

Leonaur is an imprint of Oakpast Ltd

Copyright in this form © 2016 Oakpast Ltd

ISBN: 978-1-78282-501-2 (hardcover)
ISBN: 978-1-78282-502-9 (softcover)

http://www.leonaur.com

Publisher's Notes

The views expressed in this book are not necessarily
those of the publisher.

Contents

CHAPTER 1

The True Starting Point for a History of the Army

The history of the British Army is commonly supposed to begin with the year 1661, and from the day, the 14th of February, whereon King Charles the Second took over Monk's Regiment of Foot from the Commonwealth's service to his own, and named it the Coldstream Guards. The assumption is unfortunately more convenient than accurate. The British standing army dates not from 1661 but from 1645, not from Monk's regiment but from the famous New Model, which was established by Act of the Long Parliament and maintained, in substance, until the Restoration. The continuity of the Coldstream regiment's existence was practically unbroken by the ceremony of Saint Valentine's day, and this famous corps therefore forms the link that binds the New Model to the Army of Queen Victoria.

But we are not therefore justified in opening the history of the army with the birth of the New Model. The very name indicates the existence of an earlier model, and throws us back to the outbreak of the Civil War. There then confronts us the difficulty of conceiving how an organised body of trained fighting men could have been formed without the superintendence of experienced officers. We are forced to ask whence came those officers, and where did they learn their profession. The answer leads us to the Thirty Years' War and the long struggle for Dutch Independence, to the English and Scots, numbered by tens, nay, hundreds of thousands, who fought under Gustavus Adolphus and Maurice of Nassau. Two noble regiments still abide with us as representatives of these two schools, a standing record of our army's 'prentice years.

But though we go back two generations before the Civil War to find the foundation of the New Model Army, it is impossible to pause there. In the early years of Queen Elizabeth's reign we are brought face to face with an important period in our military history, with a break in old traditions, an unwilling conformity with foreign standards, in a word, with the renascence in England of the art of war. For there were memories to which the English clung with pathetic tenacity, not in Elizabeth's day only but even to the midst of the Civil War, the memories of King Harry the Fifth, of the Black Prince, of Edward the Third, and of the unconquerable infantry that had won the day at Agincourt, Poitiers, and Creçy. The passion of English sentiment over the change is mirrored to us for all time in the pages of Shakespeare; for no nation loves military reform so little as our own, and we shrink from the thought that if military glory is not to pass from a possession into a legend, it must be eternally renewed with strange weapons and by unfamiliar methods. This was the trouble which afflicted England under the Tudors, and she comforted herself with the immortal prejudice that is still her mainstay in all times of doubt,

> *I tell thee herald,*
> *I thought upon one pair of English legs*
> *Did march three Frenchmen.*

The origin of the new departures in warfare must therefore be briefly traced through the Spaniards, the Landsknechts, and the Swiss, and the old English practice must be followed to its source. Creçy gives us no resting-place, for Edward the Third's also was a time of military reform; the next steps are to the Battle of Falkirk, the Statute of Winchester, and the Assize of Arms; and still the English traditions recede before us, till at last at the Conquest we can seize a great English principle which forced itself upon the conquering Normans, and ultimately upon all Europe.

This then is the task that is first attempted in this book: to follow, however briefly and imperfectly, the growth of the English as a military power to the time of its first manifestation at Creçy, and onward to the supreme day of Agincourt; then through the decay under the blight of the Wars of the Roses to the revival under the Tudors, and to the training in foreign schools which prepared the way for the New Model and the Standing Army. The period is long, and the conditions of warfare vary constantly from stage to stage, but we shall find the Englishman, through all the changes of the art of war unchangeable, a splendid fighting man.

The primitive national army of the English, as of other Teutonic nations, consisted of the mass of free landowners between the ages of sixteen and sixty; it was called in the Karolingian legislation by the still existing name of *landwehr*, and known in England as the *fyrd*. Its term of service was fixed by custom at two months in the year. The force was reorganised by King Alfred or by his son through the division of the country into military districts, every five hides of land being required to provide an armed man at the king's summons, and to provide him with victuals and with pay. Further, all owners of five hides of land and upwards were required to do thane's service, that is to say, to appear in the field as heavily-armed men at their own charge, and to serve for the entire campaign. The organisation of the thanes was by shires. With the conquest of England by Canute a new military element was introduced by the establishment of the royal body-guard, a picked force of from three to six thousand Danish troops, which were retained by him after the rest of the army had been sent back to Denmark, and were known as the house-*carles*.

It was with an army framed on this model—the raw levies of the *fyrd* and the better trained men of the bodyguard—that King Harold, flushed with the victory of Stamford Bridge, marched down to meet the invasion of William of Normandy. The heavily-armed troops wore a shirt of ringed or chain-mail, and a conical helmet with a bar protecting the nose; their legs were swathed in bandages not wholly unlike the "putties" of the present day, and their arms were left free to swing the Danish axe. They carried also a sword, five missile darts, and a shield, but the axe was the weapon that they loved, for the Teutonic races, unlike the Latin, have ever preferred to cut rather than to thrust. The light-armed men, who could not afford defensive armour, came into the field with spear and shield only. Yet the force was homogeneous in virtue of a single custom, wherein lies the secret of the rise of England's prowess as a military nation. Though the wealthy thanes might ride horses on the march, they dismounted one and all for action, and fought, even to the king himself, on their own feet. (An alien captain of the garrison of Hereford tried in 1055 to break through this custom. "*Anglos contra morem in equis pugnare jussit*"—*Hewitt*, vol. i.).

The force was divided into large bands or battalions, of which the normal formation for battle was a wedge broadening out from a front of two men to a base of uncertain number; the officers and the better armed men forming the point, backed by a dense column of inferior troops. It was with a single line of such wedges, apparently from five-

and twenty to thirty of them, that Harold took up his position to bar the advance of the Norman army. Having no cavalry, he had resolved to stand on the defensive, and had chosen his ground with no little skill. His line occupied the crest of a hill, his flanks were protected by ravines, and he had dug across the plain on his front a trench which was sufficient to check a rapid advance of cavalry. Moreover, he had caused each battalion to ring itself about with sharp stakes, planted into the ground at intervals with the points slanting outwards, as a further protection against the attack of horse. (This seems to be the simplest and likeliest solution of the problem of the palisade, which has provoked such acrimonious controversy—see *Kohler*, vol. i.). The reader should take note of these stakes, for he will find them constantly reappearing up to the seventeenth century.

There then the English waited in close compact masses, a wall of shields within a hedge of stakes, the men of nine-and-twenty shires under a victorious leader. There is no need to enter into details of the battle. The English, as has been well said, (*Oman*), were subjected to the same trial as the famous squares at Waterloo, alternate rain of missiles and charges of cavalry, and as yet they were unequal to it. Harold's orders had been that not a man should move, but when the Normans, after many fruitless attacks, at last under William's direction simulated flight, the order was forgotten and one wing broke its ranks in headlong pursuit of the fugitives. Possibly, if Harold had been equal to the occasion, a general advance might have saved the day, but he made no such effort, and he was in the presence of a man who overlooked no blunder. The pursuing wing was enveloped by the Normans and annihilated; and then William turned the whole of his force against the fragment of the line that remained upon the hill. The English stood rooted to the ground enduring attack after attack, until at last, worn out with fatigue and choked with dead and wounded, they were broken and cut down, fighting desperately to the end. Indiscipline had brought ruin to the nation; and England now passed, to her great good fortune, under the sway of a race that could teach her to obey.

But the English had still one more lesson to learn. Many of the nobles, chafing against the rule of a foreigner, forsook their country and, taking service with the Byzantine emperors, joined the famous Varangian Guard of the Emperor Alexius Comnenus. At Durazzo they for the second time met the Normans, under the command of Robert Guiscard. True to their custom, they dismounted and fought on foot, a magnificent corps, the choicest of the whole army. As at Hastings, the

Normans attacked and were repulsed, and as at Hastings, the undisciplined English broke their ranks in pursuit. Robert Guiscard saw his opportunity, hurled his cavalry on to their flank, and then surrounding them on all sides cut them down, in spite of a furious resistance, to the very last man. So perished these untameable, unteachable spirits, the last of the unconquered English.

The Conquest was immediately followed by the institution of knight-service. But this system, as introduced into England, differed in many material respects from that which reigned on the continent of Europe. It was less distinctly military in character, and far less perfect as an organisation for national defence. The distribution of England into knight's fees, however clearly it might be mapped out on paper, was a work of time and not to be accomplished in a day. Moreover, there was disloyalty to be reckoned with; for the English were a stiff-necked people, and were not readily reconciled to the yoke of their new masters. We find, therefore, that in very early days the practice of accepting money in lieu of personal service crept in, and enabled the Norman kings to fight their battles with hired mercenaries. For this reason England has been called the cradle of the soldier; the soldier being the man who fights for pay, *solde*, *solidus*, or, as we may say by literal translation of the Latin, the man who fights for a shilling.

The sole military interest therefore of the reigns of the Norman kings is to follow the breakdown of the feudal system for military purposes, and the rapid reversion to the Saxon methods and organisation. William Rufus was the first to appeal to the English to arm in his cause, and he did so twice with success. But in the seventh year of his reign he played them a trick which lost him their confidence for ever. The *fyrd* had furnished twenty thousand men for service against the Norman rebels in France, and had provided every man, at the cost of his shire, with ten shillings for the expenses of his journey or, to use a later expression, for his conduct-money. William met them at the rendezvous, took their two hundred thousand shillings from them to hire mercenaries withal, and dismissed them to their homes. This Rufus has been selected by an historian of repute as the earliest example of an officer and a gentleman; he should also be remembered as the first officer who set the fashion, soon to become sadly prevalent, of misappropriating the pay of his men. The reader should note in passing this early instance of conduct-money, for we shall find in it the germ of the Queen's shilling.

The reign of Henry the First is interesting in that it shows us Eng-

PLAN OF BATTL

E OF HASTINGS.

lish knights serving in the field against Robert of Normandy under the walls of Tenchbrai, (1106). We find that the old order of battle, the single line of Hastings, has disappeared and has given place to the three lines of the Byzantine school, but that, strange to say, the Saxons have forced their peculiar principle upon the Normans. (A single line of course must not be understood as a single rank, it was a line of wedges or, as we should now say, a line of columns). Henry caused his English and Norman knights to dismount, formed them into a solid battalion and placed himself at their head, keeping but one small body still on their horses. The enemy's cavalry attacked Henry's mounted men and dispersed them; but the phalanx of the dismounted remained unbroken, pressed on against the rabble of hostile infantry, broke it down and almost annihilated it. The victory was hailed by the English as atonement for the defeat at Hastings, so bitter even then was the rivalry between ourselves and our gallant neighbours across the channel.

Ten years later, (1116), the English were again in France, fighting not only against rebellious Norman barons but against their ally, the French King Louis the Sixth. A long and desultory war was closed by the action of Brenville, (25th March 1125). Again Henry dismounted four hundred out of five hundred of his knights and following the tactics of Tenchbrai won, though not without hard fighting, a second victory. A third engagement, known as the Battle of Beaumont, saw the old English practice repeated for the third time with signal success; but here must be noticed the entry of a new force, a company of archers, which contributed not a little to the fortunate issue of the day. For as the Norman cavalry came thundering down on the English battalion, the archers moved off to their left flank and poured in such a shower of arrows that the horsemen were utterly overthrown. These archers must not be confounded with the famous English bowmen of a later time, for most probably they were merely copied, like the order of battle, from the Byzantine model; but they taught the English the second of two useful lessons.

Henry had already discovered that dismounted knights could hold their own against the impetuous cavalry of France; he now learned that the attack of horse could be weakened almost to annihilation by the volley of archers. This, at a time when cavalry held absolute supremacy in war, was a secret of vital importance, a secret indeed which laid the foundation of our military power. Henry, evidently alive to it, encouraged the practice of archery by ordaining that, if any man should by accident slay another at the butts, the misadventure should not be reckoned to him as a crime.

The miserable reign of Stephen, so unsatisfactory to the general historian, possesses through the continued development of English tactical methods a distinct military interest. The year 1138 is memorable for the Battle of the Standard, the first of many actions fought against the Scots, and typical of many a victory to come. The English knights as usual fought on foot, and aided by archers made havoc of the enemy. Here is already the germ of the later infantry; we shall find lances and bows give way to pikes and muskets, but for five whole centuries we shall see the foot compounded of two elements, offensive and defensive, until the invention of the bayonet slowly welds them into one. At the Battle of Lincoln, (1141), on the other hand, we find the defensive element acting alone and suffering defeat, though not disgrace; for the dismounted knights who stood round Stephen fought with all the old obstinacy and yielded only to overwhelming numbers. Thus, though two generations had passed since the Conquest, the English methods of fighting were still in full vigour, and the future of English infantry bade fair to be assured.

Nor was the cavalry neglected; for amid all the earnest of this turbulent reign there was introduced the mimic warfare known as the tournament. This was an invention of the hot-blooded, combative French, and had been originally so close an imitation of genuine battle, that the Popes had intervened to prohibit the employment therein of any but blunt weapons. The tournament being not a duel of man against man, but a contest of troop against troop, was a training not only for individual gallantry, but for tactics, drill, discipline, and leadership; victory turning mainly on skilful handling and on the preservation of compact order. Thus by the blending of English foot and Norman horse was laid, earlier than in any other country of Europe, the foundation of an army wherein both branches took an equal share of work in the day of action.

The next in succession of our kings was a great soldier and a great administrator, yet the work that he did for the army was curiously mixed. Engaged as he was incessantly in war, he felt more than others the imperfection of the feudal as a military system. The number of knights that could be summoned to his standard was very small, and was diminished still further by constant evasion of obligations. He therefore regulated the commutation of personal military service for payment in money, and formed it, under the old name of scutage, into

Battle of Lincoln

a permanent institution. Advantage was generally taken of the system, and with the money thus obtained he took Brabançon mercenaries, the prototypes of the *landsknechts* of a later time, permanently into his pay. When he needed the feudal force to supplement these mercenaries, he fell back on the device of ordering every three knights to furnish and equip one of their number for service; and finally, driven to extremity, he re-established the old English *fyrd* as a National Militia by the Assize of Arms, (1181). This, the earliest of enactments for the organisation of our national forces, and the basis of all that followed down to the reign of Philip and Mary, contained the following provisions:—

> Every holder of one knight's fee shall have a coat of mail, (made of rings or scales of iron sewn on to leather), a helmet, a shield, and a lance; and every knight as many coats of mail, helmets, shields, and lances as there are fees in his domain.
>
> Every free layman having in chattels or rent to the value of sixteen marks shall keep the same equipment.
>
> Every free layman having in chattels or rent ten marks, shall keep an habergeon, (a similar but smaller coat without sleeves), a chaplet, (an iron scull-cap without visor), of iron, and a lance.
>
> All burgesses and the whole community of freemen shall have a wambais, (a doublet padded with cotton, wool or hair, and generally covered with leather), a chaplet of iron, and a lance.

It is noteworthy that neither the bow nor the axe appear in this list of the national weapons, an omission for which it is difficult to account, since the bow was evidently in full use at the time. Possibly the temptation to employ it for purposes of poaching may have been so strong as to make the authorities hesitate to enjoin the keeping of a bow in every poor freeman's house. The influence of the poacher will be found equally potent when the time comes for the introduction of firearms.

Richard the Lion-Heart, like his predecessors, preferred to employ mercenaries for his wars, while even the knights who accompanied him to the Crusade were in receipt of pay. Were it not that his achievements in the Holy Land had left little mark on English military history they would be well worthy of a detailed narrative, for Richard was beyond dispute a really great soldier, a good engineer, and a remarkably able commander. The story of his march from Joppa to Jerusalem and of his victory at Arsouf is known to few, but it remains to all time an example of consummate military skill. A mixed force compounded of many nations is never very easy to control, and it was doubly difficult when the best of it was composed of knights who hated the very name of subordination.

Yet it was with such material, joined to a huge body of half-disciplined infantry, that Richard executed a flank march in the presence of the most formidable of living generals, and repulsed him brilliantly when he ventured, at an extremely trying moment, to attack. The plan of the campaign, the arrangements and orders for the march, the drill and discipline imposed on the knights, and the handling of the troops in the action are all alike admirable. Yet, as has been already stated, the lessons of the Crusades wrought little influence in England, mainly because she had already learned from her own experience the value of a heavily armed infantry, and of the tactical combination of missile and striking weapons. In the rest of Europe they were for a time remembered but very soon forgotten, (the mortality among horses and the difficulty of obtaining remounts frequently forced the crusading knights to fight afoot); and England was then once more left alone with her secret.

Two small relics of the Crusades must however find mention in this place. The first is the employment of the cross as a mark for distinguishing the warriors of different nations, which became in due time the recognised substitute for uniform among European soldiers. Each nation took a different colour for its cross, that of the English being at first white, which, curiously enough, is now the regular facing for English regiments of infantry. The second relic is the military band which, there seems to be little doubt, was copied from the Saracens. In their armies trumpets and drums, the latter decidedly an Oriental instrument, were used to indicate a rallying-point; for though at ordinary times the standards sufficed to show men the places of their leaders, yet in the dust of battle these were often hidden from sight; and it was therefore the rule to gather the minstrels (such was the English term) around the standards, and bid them blow and beat strenuously and unceasingly during the action. The silence of the band was taken as a proof that a battalion had been broken and that the colours were in danger; and the fashion lasted so long that even in the seventeenth century the bandsmen in all pictures of battles are depicted, drawn up at a safe distance and energetically playing.

The reign of King John accentuated still further the weak points of the English feudal system as a military organisation. The principle introduced by the Conqueror had been to claim for the sovereign direct feudal authority over every landholder in the country, suffering no intermediate class of virtually independent vassals, such as existed in France, to intercept the service of those who owed duty to him. Of the advantages of this innovation mention shall presently be made elsewhere, but at this point it is necessary to dwell only on its military defects. The whole efficiency of the feudal system turned on the creation of a caste of warriors; and such a caste can obviously be built up only by the grant of certain exclusive privileges.

The English knights possessed no such privileges. There were no special advantages bound up with the tenure of a fief. Far from enjoying immunity from taxation, as in France and Germany, the knights were obliged to pay not only the imposts required of all classes, but scutage into the bargain. Again the winning of a knight's fee lay open to all ranks of freemen, so that it could not be regarded as the hereditary possession of a proud nobility. Yet again, the grant of the honour of knighthood was the exclusive right of the sovereign, who converted it simply into an instrument of extortion. Briefly, there was no inducement to English knights faithfully to perform their service; the sovereign took everything and gave nothing; and at last they would endure such oppression no longer.

When John required a feudal force, in the year 1205, he was obliged to arrange that every ten knights should equip one of their number for service. Moreover, the knights who did serve him showed no merit; the English contingent at Bouvines having covered itself with anything but glory, (1214). Finally, came mutiny and rebellion and the Great Charter, wherein the express stipulation that fiefs should be both alienable and divisible crushed all hopes of an hereditary caste of warriors for ever.

After the Charter the national force was composed nominally of three elements, the tenants in chief with their armed vassals, the minor tenants in chief, and the freemen subject to the Assize of Arms, the last two being both under the orders of the sheriffs. It made an imposing show on paper, but was difficult to bring efficient into the field. No man was more shameless than Henry the Third in forcing knighthood, for the sake of the fees, upon all free landholders whom he thought rich enough to support the dignity; yet, when the question became one not of money but of armed men, he was forced to fall back on the same resource as his greater namesake. He simply issued a writ for the enforcement of the Assize of Arms, (1252), and ordered the sheriffs to furnish a fixed contingent of men-at-arms, to be provided by the men of the county who were subject thereto.

The defects of feudal influence in military matters were now so manifest, that Edward the First tried hard to do away with them altogether. Strictly speaking the feudal force was summoned by a special writ addressed to the barons, ordering them to appear with their due proportion of men and horses, and by similar directions to the sheriffs to warn the tenants in chief within their bailiwicks. The system was however, so cumbrous and ineffective that Edward superseded it, (1282), by issuing commissions to one or two leading men of the county to muster and array the military forces. These Commissions of Array, as they were called, will come before us again so late as in the reign of Charles the First.

But, like all his predecessors, Edward was careful to cherish the national militia which had grown out of the *fyrd*. The Statute of Winchester, (1285), re-enacted the Assize of Arms and redistributed the force into new divisions armed with new weapons. The wealthiest class of freemen was now required to keep a hauberk of iron, a sword and a knife, and a horse. The two lower classes were now subdivided into four, whereof the first was to keep the same arms as the wealthiest, the horse excepted; the second a sword, bow and arrows, and a knife; the third battle-axes, knives, and "other less weapons," in which last are included bills; and the rest bows and arrows, or if they lived in the forest, bows and bolts, the latter being probably less deadly to the king's deer than arrows.

★★★★★★

The hauberk was a complete suit of mail, a hood joined to a jacket with sleeves, breeches, stockings, shoes and gauntlets of double chain-mail.

A bill was a broad curved blade mounted at the end of a seven-foot shaft, sometimes with a point and a hook added.

★★★★★★

Here then was the axe of Harold's day revived, and the archers established by statute. It is evident, from the fact that they wore no defensive armour, that the archers were designed to be light infantry, swift and mobile in their limbs, skilful and deadly with their weapons. The name of Edward the First must be ever memorable in our history for the encouragement that he gave to the long-bow; but we seek in vain for the man, if such there was, who founded the tradition, still happily strong among us, that the English whatever their missile weapon shall always be good shots. Even at the siege of Messina by Richard the First the archers drove the Sicilians from the walls; "for no man could look out of doors but he would have an arrow in his eye before he could shut it."

The bowmen had not long been a statutory force before they were called upon for active service. The defeat of the English by William Wallace at Cambuskenneth, (1297), had summoned Edward from France to take the field in person against the Scots; and he met them on the field of Falkirk, (1298). The Scottish Army consisted, for the most part of infantry armed with pikes, not yet the long pikes of eighteen feet which they were to wield so gallantly under Gustavus Adolphus, but still a good and formidable weapon. Wallace drew them up behind a marsh in four circular battalions ringed in with stakes, posting his light troops, which were armed principally with the short-bow, in the intervals between them, and his one weak body of horse in rear. The English knights were formed as usual in column of three divisions, vanguard, battle and rearguard, and with them was a strong force of archers.

Untrue to its old traditions, the English cavalry did not dismount, but galloped straight to the attack. The first division plunged head-long into the swamp (for the mediaeval knight, in spite of a hundred warnings, rarely took the trouble to examine the ground before him), did no execution, and suffered heavy loss. The second division, under the Bishop of Durham, then skirted the swamp and came in sight of the Scottish horse. The bishop hesitated and called a halt. "Back to your mass, bishop," answered one contemptuous knight. His comrades charged, dispersed the Scottish cavalry, and drove away the archers be-tween the pikemen; but the four battalions stood firm and unbroken, and the knights surged round them in vain. Then the king brought up the archers and the third division of horse. Pushing the archers forward, he held the cavalry back in support until an incessant rain of arrows had riddled the Scottish battalions through and through, and then hurling the knights forward into the broken ranks, he fairly swept them from the field. It was the old story, heavy fire of artillery followed by charges of cavalry, the training of the Scots as Hastings had been of the English, for the trial of Waterloo.

It is interesting to note that Edward made an effort even then for the constitutional union of the two countries which had so honour-ably lost and won the day at Falkirk, but he was four centuries before

LONGBOWMAN

his time. The war continued with varying fortune during the ensuing years. The maker of the English archers died, and under his feeble son the English Army learned at Bannockburn, (1314), an ignominious lesson in tactics. The Scotch army, forty thousand strong, was composed principally of pikemen, who were drawn up, as at Falkirk, in four battalions, with the burn in their front and broken ground on either flank. Their cavalry, numbering a thousand, a mere handful compared to the host of the English men-at-arms, was kept carefully in hand.

Edward opened the action by advancing his archers to play on the Scottish infantry, but omitted to support them; and Bruce, seeing his opportunity, let loose his thousand horse on their flank and rolled them up in confusion. The English cavalry then dashed in disorder against the serried pikes, failed, partly from want of space and partly from bad management, to make the slightest impression on them, and were driven off in shameful and humiliating defeat. So the English learned that their famous archers could not hold their own against cavalry without support, and they took the lesson to heart.

★★★★★★

Mr. Oman (*Art of War in the Middle Ages*) holds the opinion that to force a line of long-bowmen by a mere front attack was a task almost as hopeless for cavalry as the breaking of a modern square, and would have it that archers needed support on their flanks only. With all respect I must reject this view, as opposed alike to history and common sense.

★★★★★★

The old system of dismounting the men-at-arms had been for the moment abandoned with disastrous results; the man who was to revive it had been born at Windsor Castle just two years before the fight.

Thirteen years later, (1327), this boy ascended the throne of England as King Edward the Third, and almost immediately marched with a great host against the Scots. The campaign came to an end without any decisive engagement, but on the one occasion when an action seemed imminent, the English men-at-arms dismounted and put off their spurs after the old English fashion. Peace was made, but only to be broken by the Scots, and then Edward took his revenge for Bannockburn at Halidon Hill, (1333). The English men-at-arms alighted from their horses, and were formed into four battalions, each of them flanked by wings of archers, the identical formation adopted two centuries later for the pikemen and musketeers. The Scots, whose num-

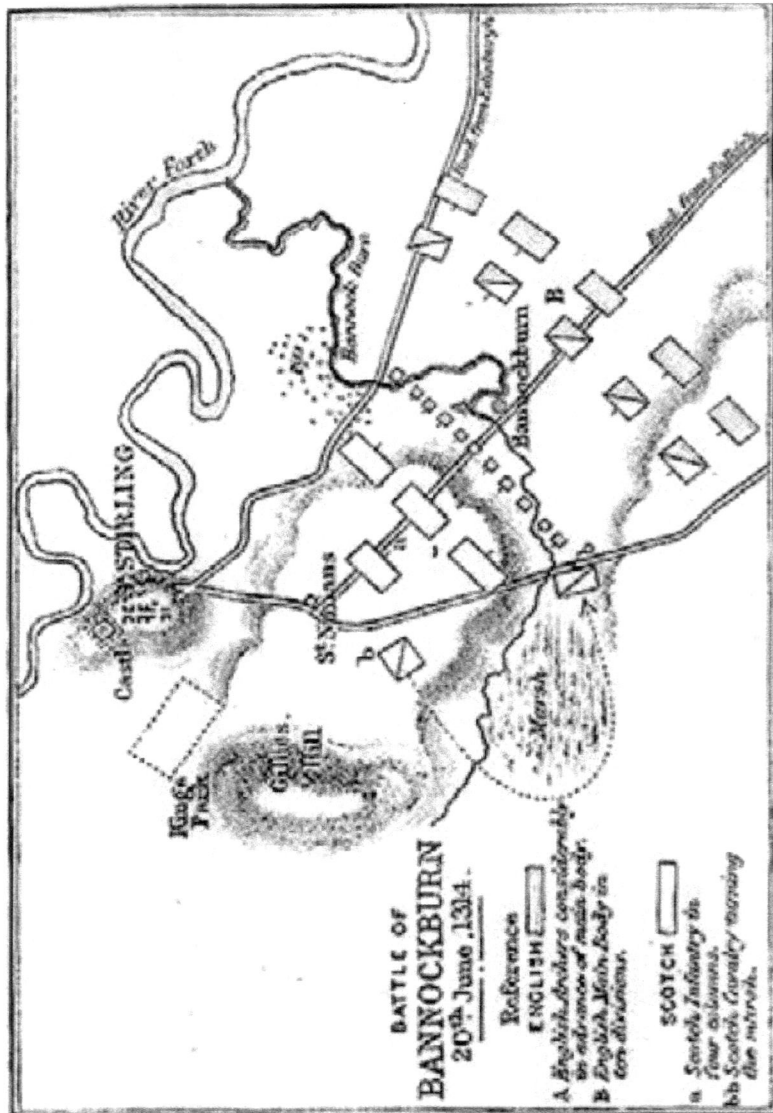

BATTLE OF
BANNOCKBURN
20th June 1314.

Reference
ENGLISH

A. English Archers considerably
in advance of main body.

B. English Main Body in
ten divisions.

SCOTCH

a. Scotch Infantry in
four columns.

bb. Scotch Cavalry turning
the retreat.

bers were far superior, were also formed on foot in four battalions, but without the strength of archers.

The old historian, (Barnes) says:

> And then, the English minstrels blew aloud their trumpets and sounded their pipes and other instruments of martial music, and marched furiously to meet the Scots.

The archers shot so thick and fast that the enemy, unable to endure it, broke their ranks, and then the English men-at-arms leaped on to their horses for the pursuit. The Scotch strove gallantly to rally in small bodies, but they were borne down or swept away; they are said to have lost ten thousand slain out of sixty thousand that entered the battle.

The mounting of the men-at-arms for the pursuit gave the finishing touch to the English tactical methods, and the nation was now ready for war on a grander scale. Moreover, there was playing round the knees of good Queen Philippa a little boy of three years old who was destined to be the victor of Poitiers. It is therefore time, while the quarrel which led to the Hundred Years' War is maturing, to observe the point to which two centuries and a half of progress had brought English military organisation.

CHAPTER 2

The System of Hiring Arms by Indent

Attention has already been called to the defects of the feudal system for military purposes, and to the shifts whereby successive sovereigns sought to make them good. With Edward the Second resort was made to a new device. Contracts, or as they were called indents, were concluded by the King with men of position, whereby the latter, as though they had been apprentices to a trade, bound themselves to serve him with a force of fixed strength during a fixed term at a fixed rate of wages. In some respects this was simply a reversion to the old practice of hiring mercenaries; but as Edward the Third placed his contracts for the most part within his kingdom, the force assumed a national character.

The current ideas of organisation were still so imperfect that the contractors generally engaged themselves to provide a mixed force of all arms; but as they naturally raised men where they could most easily get hold of them, that is to say in their own neighbourhoods, there was almost certainly some local or personal feeling to help to keep them together. For the rest the contractor of course made his own arrangements for the interior economy of his own particular troops, and enjoyed in consequence considerable powers, which descended to the colonels of a later day and have only been stripped from them within the last two generations. It is not difficult to imagine that men thus enlisted should presently, when released from national employment, have sold their services to the highest bidder and become, as they presently did become, *condottièri*. (William of Ypres, who came to England in the pay of Stephen in 1138, is reckoned the first of the *condottièri*). It is characteristic of the commercial genius of our race that England should be the cradle not only of the soldier but of the *condottière*; in other words, that she should have set the example in making warfare first a question of wages, and next a question of profit. But her work did not end here; for these reforms created the race of professional soldiers and through them the renascence of the Art of War. In short, with the opening of the Hundred Years' War the British army quickens in the womb of time, and the feudal force sinks into ever swifter decay.

But there is another side to this picture of feudal inefficiency. Moral not less than physical force is a mighty factor in war; and it Was precisely the military defects of the English feudal system that first made her a military power. Though the growth of a caste of warriors was checked, it was to make room for that which was worthy to overshadow it, a fighting nation. For in England there was not, as in other countries, any denial of civil rights to the commons of the realm. Below the ranks of the peerage all freemen enjoyed equality before the law; nay, the peerage itself conferred no privilege except on those who actually possessed it, the sons of peers being commoners, not as elsewhere noble through the mere fact of their birth.

In England there were and are nobility and gentry: in other countries nobility and gentry were merged in a single haughty exclusive caste, and between them and other freemen was fixed a great and impassable gulf. Thus the highest and the lowest of the freemen were in touch with each other in England as nowhere else in Europe. More than two centuries later than Creçy, so great and gallant a gentleman as Bayard could refuse with disdain to fight by the side of infantry. In England, whatever the pride of race, the son of the noblest peer in the land stood shoulder to shoulder with his equal when the archer fell in by his side, and where the son stood the father could feel it no shame to stand. No other nation as yet could imitate this; no other could recall a Hastings where all classes had stood afoot in one battalion. Other nations could indeed, when taught by experience, dismount their knights and align cross-bowmen with them, just as at this day they can erect an upper and lower chamber and speak of a constitution on the English model; but then as now it was the form only, not the substance, that was English.

So far for the commercial and political influence that helped to mould our military system; there remains yet another great moral force to be reckoned with. Chivalry, which had been growing slowly in England since the Third Crusade, burst in the fourteenth century into late but magnificent blossom. The nation woke to the beauty of a service which gave dignity to man's fighting instincts, which taught that it was not enough for him to be without fear if he were not also without reproach, and that though the government of the world must always rest upon force, yet mercy and justice may go hand in hand with it. The girding on of the sword was no longer a social but a religious act; it marked not merely the young man's entrance into public life, but his ordination to a great and noble function. Concurrently there had arisen a sense of the charm of glory and adventure. Hitherto the English knights had gained no repute in Europe. Hatred and jealousy had held the Saxon aloof from his Norman master; now there was no more Saxon and Norman, but the English, united and strong, a fighting people that thirsted for military fame.

Let us now briefly consider the composition and organisation of the armies that were to work such havoc in France. The cavalry was drawn for the most part from the wealthier classes, though, as has been seen, there was one division of the freemen under the statute of Winchester which was called upon to do mounted service. The more important branch, the men-at-arms, was composed of two elements, knights and squires. From the first institution of the feudal system, the number of men required from the greater vassals had forced them to equip their sons and serving-men, who after many changes were finally in the thirteenth century merged together under the generic name of *servientes*, a term which was soon corrupted into its present form of sergeants.

In the year 1294 these *servientes* were dignified by the higher title of *servientes equites*, mounted sergeants, which was six years later abandoned for the familiar name of squires. These squires must not, however, be confounded with a different class of the same appellation, namely, the apprentices who were the personal attendants of the knights. The squire of which I now speak was rather a knight of inferior order corresponding to the *bachelier* (*bas chevalier*) of France. The word knight itself gives us a hint of this inferiority, being the same as the German *knecht*, whereas *ritter* is the German term that expresses what is generally understood as a knight in English. The inner history of chivalry is the story of the struggle of the sergeants to rise to an equality with the knights of the first order, and in the fourteenth century they were not far from their goal. Even now they were considered the backbone of the English Army, and were equipped in all points like the class above them.

Men-at-arms, an expression derived from the French, were so called because they were covered with defensive armour from top to toe; but as the middle of the fourteenth century is a period of transition in the development of armour, it is difficult to describe their equipment with any certainty. Their offensive arms were the lance, sword, dagger, and shield. Trained from very early youth in the handling of weapons they were doubtless proficient enough with them; but they do not seem to have been great horsemen, and indeed it is recorded that they were sometimes tied to the saddle. Monstrelet, writing in the year 1416, tells us of the astonishment which certain Italians created among the French because they could actually turn their horses at the gallop. It is probable that the bits employed were too weak, and that the cumbrousness of the saddle and the weight carried by each man were sad obstacles to good horsemanship; but it is worth remembering in any case that, as this passage plainly shows, men-at-arms in the saddle were reduced to one of two alternatives, to move slowly and retain control of their horses, or to gallop for an indefinite period wherever the animals might choose to carry them.

The favourite horses, alike for speed, endurance, and courage, were the Spanish, which, as they could only reach England by the journey overland through France, were not always very easily obtained. Philip the Bold in 1282 refused to allow one batch of eighty such horses to be transhipped to England; but from a contract still extant, of the year 1333, it appears that Edward the Third still counted on Spain to provide him with remounts. These horses, however, were only bestridden for action, being committed on the march to the care of the shield-bearers or squires, who led them, as was natural, on their right-hand side, and thus procured for them the curious name of *dextrarii*, (whence the French word *destrier*). The usual allowance of horses for a knight was three, besides a packhorse for his baggage, the smallest of which, named the palfrey, was that which he rode on ordinary occasions; in fact, to put the matter into modern language, a knight started on a campaign with a first charger, a second charger, and a pony. The first charger was always a stallion; the rest might be geldings or mares. From the year 1298 the practice of covering horses with defensive armour was introduced into England, an equipment which soon came to be regarded as so essential that one branch of the cavalry, and that the most important, was reckoned by the number of barded horses.

The personal retinue of the knights was made up of apprentices or aspirants to the rank which they held. The squire or shield-bearer took charge of the knight's armour on the march, and was responsible for maintaining it in proper order; and it is worth remarking that the English squire took a pride in burnishing the metal to the highest pitch of brilliancy, thus early establishing those traditions of smartness which are still so strong in our cavalry. It was also the squire's duty, among many others, to help his master to don his harness when the time for action came, beginning with his iron shoes or sollerets, and working upwards till the fabric was crowned by the iron headpiece, and the finishing touch added by the assumption of the shield. The reader will readily understand that a really efficient squire must have been invaluable, for if an engagement came in any way as a surprise there was an immediate rush for the baggage, and a scene of confusion that must have beggared description. Fortunately, the fact that both sides were generally alike unready, and the punctiliousness of chivalric courtesy, permitted as a rule ample time not only for the equipment of all ranks, but for the marshalling of the host.

In the matter of administrative organisation the men-at-arms were distributed into constabularies, being commanded by officers called constables. The strength of a constabulary seems to have varied from five-and-twenty to eighty; and this variety, together with the absence of any tactical unit of fixed strength, makes it impossible to state how many constabularies were included in the next tactical division. This was called the banner, and was commanded by a banneret, a rank originally conferred only upon such as could bring a certain number of followers into the field. Promotion to the degree of banneret was marked by cutting off the forked tail of the pennon which was carried by the ordinary knight, and leaving the remnant square. So at the present day, the pennons of lances are forked, the square being reserved for the standards of squadrons and regiments.

The independent employment of small bodies in action was almost unknown, the rule being to pack an indefinite number of men-at-arms, hundreds or even thousands, into a close and solid mass, its depth almost if not quite as great as its frontage. The *haye*, or thin line, is of much later date. Ordinarily some modification of the wedge was the formation preferred; that is to say, that the frontage of the front rank was somewhat less than that of the rear; the mass of that particular shape being judged to be less liable to disorder and better adapted for breaking into a hostile phalanx. The relative strength of the front and rear ranks depended entirely on the numbers that were packed in between them, and it may readily be supposed that the evolutions which so unwieldly a body could execute were very few. Probably, until the moment of action came, sufficient space was maintained to permit every horse to turn on his own ground, after the Roman fashion, to right, left, or about; but for the attack ranks and files were closed up as tightly as possible, and all other considerations were sacrificed to the maintenance of a compact array.

It was said of the French knights who marched with Richard the Lion-heart that an apple thrown into the midst of them would not have fallen to the ground. We must therefore rid ourselves of the popular notion of the knight as a headlong galloping cavalier. The attack of men-at-arms could not be very rapid unless it were made in disorder; and though it conies strictly under the head of shock-action, the shock was rather that of a ponderous column moving at a moderate pace than of a light line charging at high speed. By bearing these facts in mind it will be easier to understand the failure of mounted men-at-arms to break a passive square of infantry.

Next after the men-at-arms came a species of cavalry called by the name of pauncenars, (from the German *panzer*, a coat of mail), which was less fully equipped with defensive armour, but wore the habergeon. (sleeveless coat of chain-mail), and was armed with the lance.

Lastly came the light cavalry of the *fyrd*, originally established to patrol the English coast. These were called hobelars, from the hobbies or ponies which they rode, and were equipped with an iron helmet, a heavily padded doublet (*aketon*), iron gloves, and a sword.

Turning next to the infantry, there were Welsh spearmen, carrying the weapon which gave them their name, but without defensive armour. Indeed it should seem that they were not overburdened with clothes of any kind, for they were every one provided at the King's expense with a tunic and a mantle, which were by express direction made of the same material and colour for all. These Welsh spearmen therefore were the first troops in the English service who were dressed in uniform, and they received it first in the year 1337. The colour of their clothing unfortunately remains unknown to us. (The earliest instance of uniform in modern Europe is found in the militia of the Flemish towns at the Battle of Courtrai, 1302 —*Köhler*).

Next we come to the peculiar strength of England, the archers. Though a certain number of them seem generally to have been mounted, yet, like the dragoons of a later day, these rode for the sake of swifter mobility only, and may rightly be reckoned as infantry. As has been already stated, the archers wore no defensive armour except an iron cap, relying on their bows alone. These bows were six feet four inches long; the arrows, of varying length but generally described as cloth-yard shafts, were fitted with barb and point of iron and fledged with the feathers of goose or peacock. But the weapon itself would have gone for little without the special training in its use wherein the English excelled. Bishop Latimer (and we may reasonably assume that in such matters there had been little change in a hundred and fifty years), says:—

> My father was diligent in teaching me to shoot with the bow; he taught me to draw, to lay my body to the bow, not to draw with strength of arm as other nations do, but with the strength of the body. I had my bows bought me according to my age and strength; as I increased in these my bows were made bigger and bigger.

★★★★★★

> The contract price of a bow in 1341 was, unpainted is., painted is. 6d.; of a sheaf of twenty-four arrows is. 2d. An archer's pay was 3d. a day.

★★★★★★

The principle was in fact analogous to that which is taught to young oarsmen at the present day. The results of this training were astonishing. The range of the longbow in the hands of the old archers is said to have been fully two hundred and forty yards, and the force of the arrow to have been such as to pierce at a fair distance an inch of stout timber. Moreover, the shooting was both rapid and accurate. Indeed the long-bow was in the fourteenth century a more formidable weapon than the cross-bow, which had been condemned by Pope Innocent the Second as too deadly for Christian warfare so far back as 1139.

It was at no disadvantage in the matter of range, while it could be discharged far more quickly; and further, since it was held not horizontally but perpendicularly to the ground, the archers could stand closer together, and their volleys could be better concentrated. Thus the long-bow, though the crossbow was not unknown to the English, was not only the national but the better weapon. In action the archers were ranked as deep as was consistent with the delivery of effective volleys, the rear ranks being able to do good execution by aiming over the heads of the men before them. It may be imagined from the muscular training undergone by the archers that they were physically a magnificent body of men.

Strictly speaking the archers were the artillery of the army, according to the terminology of the time, (1 Samuel xx. 40), the word *artillator* being used in the time of Edward the Second to signify the officer in charge of what we now call the ordnance-stores. But to avoid confusion we must use the word in its modern sense, the more so since we find among the stores of the custodian, (Thomas de Roldeston), of the King's artillery in 1344 the items of saltpetre and sulphur for the manufacture of powder, and among his men six "gonners." Gun, it should be added, was the English, cannon the French name for these weapons from the beginning. It will presently be necessary to notice their first appearance in the field.

As to the general organisation of the army, the whole was divided into thousands under an officer called a millenar, subdivided into hundreds, each under a centenar, and further subdivided into twenties, each under a vintenar. The commander-in-chief was usually the king in person, aided by two principal officers, the high constable and the marshal, whose duties were, roughly speaking, those of adjutant and quartermaster-general. For tactical purposes the army was distributed into three divisions, called the vanguard, battle and rearguard, which kept those names whatever their position in the field or on the march, whether the host was drawn up, as most commonly, in three lines, or in one. Trumpets were used for purposes of signalling, though so far as can be gathered they sounded no distinct calls, and were dependent for their significance on orders previously issued. The failing in this respect is the more remarkable, inasmuch as the signals of the chase with the horn were already very numerous and very clearly and accurately defined.

The pay of all ranks can fortunately be supplied from the muster-roll of Calais in 1346, and although I shall not again encumber these pages with a pay-list I shall for once print it entire:

The Prince of Wales	20s.	a day
The Bishop of Durham	6s. 8d	,, ,,
Earls	6s. 8d	,, ,,
Barons and Bannerets	4s.	,, ,,
Knights	2s.	,, ,,
Esquires, Constables, Captains, and Leaders	1s.	,, ,,
Vintenars	6d.	,, ,,
Mounted Archers	6d.	,, ,,

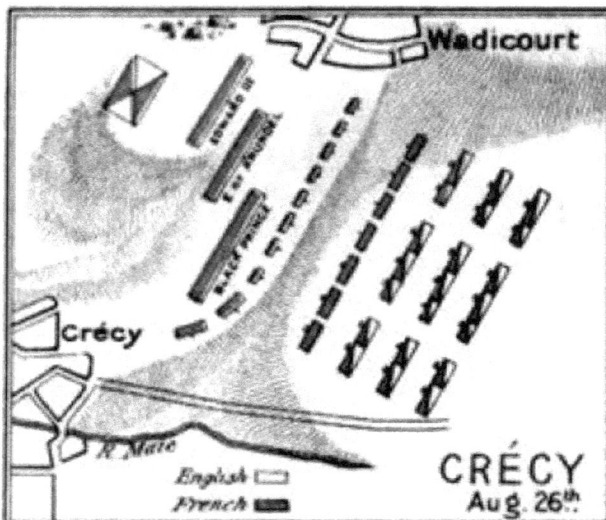

Wadicourt

Crécy

R. Mate

English ☐
French ▪

CRÉCY
Aug. 26ᵗʰ

Cherbourg

St Vaast de la Hogue

Valognes

Montebourg

St Sauveur

Carentan

Bayeux

Caen

R. Seine

St Lo

R. Orne

Falaise

Viré

Argen

CAMPAIGN OF 1346

English Miles

10   20   30   40   50

Edward the IIIrd →

the French →

Boulogne   St Omer

Aire

Agincourt

Montreuil   St Pol

Hesdin   Fréyent

Wadicourt   la Broye   Bonnières

Ruin   Crécy   Crécy   Lucheux

R. Somme   Doullans

St Valery   Noyelle

Blanche Tache   Abbeville   Forceville

Eu   Pt Rémy

Bailleul   Acheux   Hangest   Albert

Dieppe   Dismont   Picquigny

Senarpont   Amiens   Corbie

Fécamp   Aumale   Poix   Boves

Coppegheul

Grandvilliers   Dargnes

Forges

Harfleur   Gournay   St Just   Beauvais

Rouen   Clermont

Pont Audemer

Pt del Arche   Gisors   Creil

Brionne   les Andelys

Chambly

Louviers   St Jaffroy   Vernon   la Roche Guyon   Beaumont

Lisieux   Cocherel   Dacy   Pontoise   Franconville

Beaumont le Roger   Rubbedoux   Mantel   St Denis

Evreux   Poissy

Conches   St Germain   Paris

Nonancourt   St Cloud

Verneuil   Dreux   Bourg la Reine

Pauncenars	6d. „ „
Hobelars	6d. „ „
Foot-Archers	3d. „ „
Welsh Spearmen	2d. „ „
„ Vintenars	4d. „ „

Masons, Carpenters, Smiths, Engineers, Miners, Gunners, 10d., 6d. and 3d.

It is melancholy to have to record that even so early as in 1342 corruption and fraudulent dealing had begun in the army. The marshals were ordered to muster the men-at-arms once a month, and to refuse pay for men who were absent or inadequately armed or indifferently mounted. We shall see the practice of drawing pay for imaginary men and the tricks played on muster-masters increase and multiply, till they demand a special vocabulary and a certain measure of official recognition. A favourite abuse among men-at-arms was the claim of extortionate compensation for horses lost on active service, leading to an order in this same year that all horses should be valued on admission to the corps, and marked to prevent deception.

Thus early was the road opened that leads to the broad arrow. The taint of corruption, indeed, clings strongly to every army, with the possible exception of the Prussian, in Europe. War is a time of urgency and stress, which does not admit of strict audits or careful inspections, and poor human nature is too weak not to turn such an opportunity to its profit. It is an unpleasant thought that dishonesty and peculation should be inseparably associated with so much that is noble and heroic in human history, but the fact is indisputable, and must not be lightly passed over. Moreover the days when English cavalry shall go to war on their own horses may not yet be numbered; and it may be useful to remember that the mediaeval man-at-arms would mount himself on his worst animal in order to break him down the quicker, and claim for him the price of his best. It is only by constant wariness against such evils that there can be built up a sound system of military administration.

CHAPTER 3

Invasion of France by Edward III

Having now sketched the composition of the English forces, let us move forthwith to the scene of action.

We must omit the early incidents of the war, (1339), and the assumption by Edward of the famous motto wherein he consecrated his claim to the crown of France, *Dieu et mon droit*. We must pass by the famous naval action, of Sluys, (June 24, 1340), where the English commanders in their zeal to follow the precepts of Vegetius, thought it more important to have the sun in the enemy's eyes than the wind in their own favour, and where the archers, acting as marine sharp-shooters, were the true authors of the English victory.

We must overlook likewise the innumerable sieges, even that of Quesnoy, where the English first came under the fire of cannon, merely remarking that owing to their ignorance of that particular branch of warfare, the English were uniformly unsuccessful; and we must come straight to the year 1345, when Henry of Lancaster, Earl of Derby, landed at Bayonne with a force of three thousand men for a campaign in Gascony and Guienne. The name of our first artillery-officer has been given; attention must now be called to our first engineer, this same Earl of Derby, who had lately been recalled from service with the Spaniards against the Moors at the siege of Algesiras, and was the first man who taught the English how to take a fortified town.

Derby then with his little army harried Gascony and Guienne for a time, until the arrival of a superior French force compelled him to retire and gave him much ado to defend himself. Accordingly, in June 1346 Edward the Third impressed a fleet of innumerable small vessels, none of them exceeding sixty tons burden, embarked thereon four thousand men-at-arms, ten thousand archers and five or six thousand Welsh spearmen, and sailed for the coast of France. On the 12th of

July he put into St.Vaast de la Hogue, a little to the east of Cherbourg, dispersed a French force that was stationed to oppose him, and successfully effected his landing. Six days were allowed to recruit men and horses after the voyage, and the army then moved eastward to the Seine, leaving a broad line of ruin and desolation in its wake, and advanced up the left bank of the river.

King Philip of France had meanwhile collected an army at Rouen, whence he marched parallel to the English along the right bank of the Seine, crossed it at Paris, and stood ready to fall upon Edward if he should strike southward to Guienne. But Edward's plans were of the vaguest; his diversion had already relieved Derby, and he now crossed the Seine at Poissy and struck northward as if for Flanders. Philip no sooner divined his purpose than he too hastened northward, outmarched the English, crossed the Somme at Amiens, gave orders for the occupation of every bridge and ford by which the English could pass the river, and then recrossing marched straight upon Edward's right flank.

The position of the English was now most critical, for they could not cross the Somme and were fairly hemmed in between the river and the sea. At his wits' end Edward examined his prisoners, and from them learned of the ford of Blanche Tache in the tidal water about eight miles below Abbeville. Thither accordingly he marched, and after waiting part of a night for the ebb-tide, forced the passage in the teeth of a French detachment that had been stationed to guard it, and sending six officers to select for him a suitable position pursued his way northward through the forest of Creçy. On the morning of the 26th of August, 1346, he crossed the river Maie, and there swinging his front round from north to south-east he turned and stood at bay.

The position was well chosen. The army occupied a low line of heights lying between the villages of Creçy and Wadicourt, the left flank resting on a forest, the right on the River Maie. Edward ordered every man to dismount, and parked the horses and baggage waggons in an entrenched leaguer (since the Zulu war we have called it a *laager*, forgetting the English word that lay ready to our hand), in rear. The army was too weak to cover the whole line of the position, so the archers were pushed forward and extended in a multitude of battalions along the front, and backed with Welsh spearmen.

Echeloned in rear of them stood the three main divisions of the army; foremost and to the right the vanguard of twelve hundred men-at-arms under the Black Prince, next to it the battle of as many

CRÉCY
August 26th. 1346.

French Army.

⬚ Men at Arms
∴ Cross-bowmen
▨ Infantry
E.E. Genoese
F.F. Count of Alençon
G.G. Duke of Lorraine
H.H. Remainder of Army hurrying to the Front.

ROMAN ROAD

Wadicourt

Estrées

Fontaine

H

Cross of the King of Bohemia

R. Maye

To Abbeville

English Waggon-Park

Bois de la Grange

To Rue and Crotoy

Crécy

Forest of Crécy

English Army.

▲ Men-at-Arms ❃ Archers

A. Prince Edward
B. Earl of Northampton
C. The King
D. The King's Windmill

more under the Earl of Arundel, and behind it, covering the extreme left, the rearguard, consisting of fifteen hundred men-at-arms and six thousand mixed archers and infantry under the King. The country being rich in provisions Edward ordered every man to eat a hearty meal before falling into his place, for he knew that the Englishman fights best when he is full. When the host was arrayed in order he rode round the whole army to cheer it; and then the men lay down, the archers with their helmets and bows on the ground before them, and waited till the French should come.

Philip meanwhile had crossed the Somme at Abbeville on the morning of the 26th, and turned eastward in the hope of cutting off the English. Finding that he was too late, he countermarched and turned north, at the same time sending forward officers to reconnoitre. The afternoon was far advanced, and the French were wearied with a long, disorderly march when these officers returned with intelligence of the English. Philip ordered a halt, but the indiscipline and confusion were such that the order could not be obeyed. The noblest blood in France was riding on in all its pride to make an end of the despised English, and a mass of rude infantry was waiting to share the slaughter and the spoil. So they blundered on till they caught sight of the English lying quietly down in order of battle; and therewith all good resolutions vanished and Philip gave the order to attack.

It was now nearly five o'clock, and the heaven was black with clouds, which presently burst in a terrific thunderstorm. The English archers slipped off their bowstrings to keep them dry, and waited; while six thousand Genoese cross-bowmen, jaded by the long march, drenched and draggled with the rain that beat into their faces, conscious that they were almost disarmed by the wetness of their bowstrings, shuffled wearily into their stations along the French front. Their leaders complained that they were unfairly treated.

"Who cares for your rabble?" answered the Count of Alençon. "They are nothing but useless mouths, more trouble than help."

So the cross-bowmen sulkily took their position, and the rest of the French army, from twelve to twenty thousand men-at-arms and some fifteen thousand infantry, ranged themselves in three massive lines behind them. A vast flight of ravens flew over the opposing arrays, croaking loudly over the promised feast of dead men.

Then the storm passed away inland into France, and the sun low down in the west flashed out in all his glory full in the faces of the French. The Genoese advanced and raised a loud cry, thrice repeated,

CHARGE OF THE FRENCH KNIGHTS AT CRECY

to strike terror into the English: the archers over against them stood massive and silent. The loud report of two or three cannon, little more harmful than the shouts of the Genoese, was the only answer; and then the archers stepped forward and drew bow. In vain the Genoese attempted to reply; they were overwhelmed by the torrent of shafts; they shrank back, cut their bowstrings and would have fled, but for a line of French mounted men-at-arms which was drawn up in their rear to check them. The proud chivalry of France was chafing impatiently behind them, and Philip would wait no longer. "Slay me these rascals," he said brutally; and the first line of men-at-arms thundered forward, trod the hapless Genoese under foot, and pressed on within range of the arrows.

And then ensued a terrible scene. The great stallions, maddened by the pain of the keen barbed shafts, broke from all control. They jibbed, they reared, they swerved, they plunged, striking and lashing out hideously, while the rear of the dense column, carried forward by its own momentum, surged on to the top of the foremost and wedged the whole into a helpless choking mass. And still the shower of pitiless arrows fell swift as snow upon the thickest of the press; and the whole of the French fighting line became a confused welter of struggling animals, maimed cross-bowmen, and fallen cavaliers, crippled by the weight of their armour, an easy prey to the long, keen knives of the Welsh.

Nevertheless some few of the French men-at-arms had managed to pierce through the archers. The blind king of Bohemia had been guided by two faithful knights through the centre, Alençon had skirted them on one flank, the Count of Flanders on the other, and all had fallen upon the Black Prince's battalion. The danger was greatest on the left flank; but the Earl of Arundel moved up the second line of the echelon to his support, and the English held their own. Then the second line of the French advanced, broke through the archers, not without heavy loss, and fell likewise upon the English men-at-arms. The Prince of Wales was overthrown, and was only saved by the devotion of his standard-bearer, but the battalion fought on. It was probably at this time that Arundel sent a messenger to the king for reinforcements.

"Is my son dead or hurt?" he asked.

"No, sire, but he is hard beset."

"Then return to those who sent you and bid them send me no more such messages while my son is alive; tell them to let the boy win his spurs."

BATTLE OF
CRECY
26th Aug 1346

English
French

Wadicourt

Archers

Archers

KING

Archers

Archers

Valley Clipt

Park

Royal Road

Crecy Church

R. Maye

The message was carried back to the battalion, and the men-at-arms fought on stoutly as ever. The archers seem also to have rallied and closed on the flank and rear of the 1346, attacking French. Alençon's banner could still be seen August 26. swaying behind a hedge of archers, and Philip, anxious to pour his third and last line into the fight, had actually advanced within range of the arrows. But the power of the bowmen was still unweakened, the ground was choked with dead men and horses, and the light was failing fast. He yielded to the entreaties of his followers and rode from the field; and the first great battle of the English was won.

When morning dawned the country was full of straggling Frenchmen, who from the sudden change in the direction of the advance had lost all knowledge of their line of retreat; the few that retained some semblance of organised bodies were attacked and broken up. Never was victory more complete. The French left eleven great lords, eighty-three bannerets, over twelve hundred knights and some thousands of common soldiers dead on the field. It was a fortunate issue to a reckless and ill-planned campaign. It is customary to give all credit for the victory to the archers, but this is unjust. Superbly as they fought they would have been broken without the men-at-arms, even as the men-at-arms would have been overwhelmed without the archers. Both did their duty without envy or jealousy, and therein lay the secret of their success.

The siege and capture of Calais followed, and then by the mediation of the Pope peace was made, and for a time preserved. Petty hostilities however never ceased in Brittany, and finally in 1355 the war broke out anew. Three armies were fitted out,—one of a thousand men-at-arms under the Black Prince for operations in Guienne, a second under the Earl of Derby for Brittany, and a third under the personal command of the king. Little, however, was effected in the campaign of 1355. The king was recalled to England by an invasion of the Scots, and the operations of 1356 in Brittany were checked by the appearance of the French king in superior force. But at the close of July 1356 the Black Prince suddenly started on a wild raid from the Dordogne in the south to the Loire.

His object seems to have been to effect a junction with Derby's forces at Orleans; but it is difficult to see how he could have hoped for success. He had reached Vierzon on the Cher, August 28, when he heard that the King of France was on his way to meet him in overwhelming strength. Unable to retreat through the country which he had laid waste on his advance, he turned sharp to the west down the Cher and struck the Loire at Tours. There for four days he halted, for what reason it is difficult to explain, since the delay enabled the French to cross the Loire and seriously to threaten his retreat.

There was now nothing for the prince but to retire southward with all haste. The French were hard on his track, and followed him so closely that he was much straitened by want of supplies. On the 14th of September the English were at Chatelheraut and the French at La Haye, little more than ten miles apart, and on the 15th the French made a forced march which brought them fairly to southward of the prince, and between him and his base at Bordeaux. All contact however had been lost; and the French king, making sure that the prince had designs on Poitiers, swung round to the westward and moved straight upon the town. On the 17th, while in full march, his rearguard was suddenly surprised by the advanced parties of the prince. As in the movements after the Alma, each army was executing a flank march, quite unconsciously, in the presence of the other. The French rearguard pursued the reconnoitring party to the main body of the English, and after a sharp engagement was repulsed with heavy loss. The French Army had actually marched across the line of the Black Prince's retreat, and left it open to him once more.

Edward lost no time in looking for a suitable position, and presently found it at Maupertuis some fifteen miles south-west of Poitiers. There to the north of the River Miosson is a plain seamed with deep ravines running down to that stream; and behind one of these he took his stand, (Sept.18), facing north-east. The sides of the ravine were planted with vineyards and blocked by thick hedges, so that it was impossible for cavalry to cross it except by a track which was broad enough for but four horsemen abreast; and these natural advantages the prince improved by repairing all weak places in the fences and by digging entrenchments. One exposed spot on his left flank he strengthened by a leaguer of waggons as well as with the spade. He then told off his archers to line the hedges which commanded the passage across the ravine, and drew up his men-at-arms, all of them dismounted, in three lines behind it. The first line he committed to the Earls of Warwick and Suffolk, the rearmost to the Earl of Salisbury, and the centre he reserved for himself. His whole force, augmented as it was by a contingent of Gascons, did not exceed six or seven thousand men, half of whom were archers.

So passed the day of the 18th of September on the English side.

The French on their part, instead of blocking up their retreat to the south and reducing them by starvation, simply moved down from Poitiers to within a league of the English position and halted for the night. Their force amounted to sixty thousand men, and they might well feel confident as to the issue of an action. Indeed, when the Black Prince, fully alive to the desperate peril of his situation, negotiated for an evacuation of the country, they imposed such terms that he could not in honour accept them. They therefore reconnoitred the English position, and laid their plans for the morrow. Three hundred chosen men-at-arms, backed by a column of German, Italian, and Spanish knights, were to charge down the ravine upon the archers, disperse them, and attack the English men-at-arms on the other side. Three lines, each of three massive battalions containing from three to four thousand men-at-arms, with lances shortened to a length of five feet, were to follow them afoot, and the English were to be crushed by their own tactics.

It is hardly surprising that in the night the Black Prince's heart failed him. He resolved while he could to place the Miosson between him and the French, and at dawn, Sept. 19, began his retreat, leaving the rearguard, however, still in the position at Maupertuis in case withdrawal should be impossible.

★★★★★★

The only authority for this is the rhymed chronicle of the Chandos herald, but, as Köhler observes, the proceeding was so natural, and, I may add, the invention of such a story so improbable, that it is difficult not to accept it.

★★★★★★

He also sent two knights to watch the French Army, who however approached too closely to it and were captured. His first line had already crossed the Miosson when intelligence reached him that the French had advanced, and that the rearguard was engaged. He at once ordered the vanguard to return, and himself hastening back with his own division, despatched three hundred mounted men-at-arms and as many mounted archers without delay to strengthen his right wing. The French meanwhile had moved forward, gaily singing the song of Roland, to find the way blocked by the hedges and vineyards of the ravine. Undismayed they plunged down into the narrow track; and then the English archers behind the hedges opened at close range a succession of frightfully destructive volleys. The foremost of the horsemen fell headlong down, the rear plunged confusedly on the top of them, and the pass was blocked with a heaving, helpless crowd, on which the arrows hissed down in an eternal merciless shower. The supporting column of foreign cavalry was unable to act in the confusion; it was already under the fire of the archers, and before it could move the English mounted men on the right wing came down full upon its left flank, and killed or captured every man.

And now the wounded French horses, mad with pain and terror, many of them riderless and all beyond control, dashed back on to the first line of the dismounted French men-at-arms. It was a charge of mad animals, the most terrible of all charges, and the huge battalion fell into confusion before it. Edward was watching the battle keenly from his position; he had already ordered his men-at-arms to mount, and now Sir John Chandos, whose name must always be linked to Edward's as that of Collingwood to Nelson, broke out aloud with, "Forward, sire, forward, and the day is yours!"

"Aye, John," answered the prince, with a thought perhaps of the morning's retreat, "No going backward today. Forward banner, in the name of God and St. George!"

The preliminary attack of the mounted men on the right had already cleared the way for them. The English cavalry scrambled in haste down into the ravine on the right, and fell upon the French men-at-arms. The front and centre divisions, already much shaken, were easily broken and dispersed; the third and strongest still remained, and against this, which resisted desperately, the whole force of the English was turned. The lesson of Falkirk was remembered. The mounted archers made the gaps and the men-at-arms rode into them. The division was broken, the king was captured, and the mass of the fugitives making for Poitiers found the gates closed against them and were cut down by hundreds. The action began at six in the morning, and lasted till late into the afternoon. The French losses were enormous.

Over and above the king and many great lords two thousand men-at-arms were captured, and two thousand five hundred more were left dead on the field; the number of the unhappy foot-men that were slain it is impossible to state. The English loss is variously set down, the reports ranging from half the force to sixty-four men. The battle, from the disparity between the strength of the two sides, must remain ever memorable in the annals of war. To the English, who had but lately risen above the horizon as a military power, it gave a prestige that has never been lost.

The peace of Brétigny, 1360, closed the war and the English Army

THE CAMPAIGN OF 1356.

POITIERS
Oct. 19th

Scale 2½ inches a mile

English
French

Maupertius

les Bordes

Chartres

Orleans

Blois

La Haye

Chatelleraut

Poitiers

GUIENNE

Bordeaux

Limoges

R. Vienne

R. Garonne
R. Dordogne
R. Isle
R. Dronne

St. Jean d'Angely

Verteuil

Aiguillon

R. Lot

Scale of Miles

0   10   20   30   40   50   60   70   80

March of the Black Prince
French

was disbanded. But the soldiers, like the ten thousand Greeks who returned from Cunaxa, were too deeply bitten with their profession to abandon it for the tedium of peace. They therefore formed themselves into independent bodies, or Free Companies, and for years were the scourge of France, their chamber as they called it, which they plundered and ravaged at their pleasure. The greatest of their leaders was John Hawkwood, of whom something more must presently be said, but these bands, in less or greater numbers, were constantly to be found fighting for hire against the French. Thus three hundred of them fought for the King of Navarre against the King of, France at Cocherel, May 16 1364.

The numbers engaged were little. more than fifteen hundred on each side, but the action is interesting as showing the efforts of the French to meet the peculiar tactics of the English. In order to have no more trouble with unruly horses the French men-at-arms dismounted and fought on foot, and now for the first time the archers found themselves outdone. The armour of the French was so good that it turned the cloth-yard shafts; and being slightly superior in numbers the French men-at-arms forced their enemy off the field. It was but a slight success, but a defeat even of a small body of English was such a rarity in those days that it gave the French great hopes for the future, hopes which were soon to be dashed to the ground.

In the following year, 1365, a quarrel as to the succession to the Duchy of Brittany between Charles of Blois and John of Montfort brought the English again into the field. The French King Charles the Fifth sent assistance to support the former, whereupon John of Montfort at once appealed to the English. John Chandos and several more of the garrison in France, eager for fresh battle against their old enemies, asked permission to join Montfort as volunteers.

"You may go full well," answered the Black Prince. "Since the French are going for Charles of Blois, I give you good leave."

The English, both volunteers and mercenaries, accordingly hurried to the scene of war; and at Auray, Sept. 29 1365, they fought the action which decided the campaign. The numbers engaged did not exceed four thousand in either army. Both sides dismounted, and the French men-at-arms discarding the lance as unfit for fighting afoot equipped themselves with battle-axes, so that there promised to be a stubborn fight. The English archers as usual opened the engagement, but as at Cocherel their shafts could not penetrate the armour of the French; whereupon with great deliberation they threw down their bows, and boldly advancing to the French men-at-arms plucked their axes from their hands and plied the weapons against their astonished owners with terrible effect.

The whole proceeding furnishes so good an example of the thoughtless, thick-headed gallantry of the English soldier, that one can only marvel that the Battle of Auray should be practically unknown to Englishmen. The intensely ludicrous picture that can be conjured up of a series of detached struggles between the brawny active English-men in their doublets and hose, and the unhappy Frenchmen cased stiffly in their mail, the panting, the staggering, and the rattling, the agonised curses from behind the vizor, and the great broad laugh on the honest English face—this alone should have saved it from oblivion. The English men-at-arms came quickly to the support of the bowmen, and after a long and desperate engagement, for the noble and gallant Bertrand du Guesclin was in command of the French, the English drove their enemy from the field and as usual finished the pursuit on horseback. There was no question in the action of superior archery or advantage of position, though Chandos indeed handled his reserve in a masterly fashion, but it was simply a matter of what the Duke of Wellington called bludgeon-work; and at this too the English proved themselves the better men.

By this time the oppression of the Free Companies had become so insufferable, (1366), that, in order to rid the country of them, Charles the Fifth ordered Bertrand du Guesclin to take a certain number of them into service and march with them to fight for the bastard Henry of Trastamare against Pedro the Cruel of Castile. It would be a mistake, we must note in passing, to look upon these companies as composed simply of low ruffians; they seem on the contrary to have been made up largely of the class of esquires, while there were poor noblemen serving even among the archers. On entering Spain they took to themselves a white cross, the old English colour of the Crusades, as their distinctive mark, and were apparently the first English troops that introduced this substitute for uniform.

Further, they called themselves the White Company, and were in this respect the forerunners of the Buffs and Blues. They did little profitable work under du Guesclin, and were presently dismissed, just in time to be re-enlisted to the number of twelve thousand by the Black Prince, who, dreading an alliance of France with Spain, was preparing an expedition for the rescue of Peter the Cruel. The vassals of Aquitaine and Gascony were also summoned to the Prince's

Beauvoir

King of France

Orleans

Dauphin

Poictiers

Cavalry

Cavalry

Hedge

Salisbury

Warwick

Prince
of Wales

Cavalry

Hedge

Maupertuis Valley

Farm of
Maupertuis

BATTLE OF
POICTIERS
19th Sept. 1356
½ Mile

English

French

standard, a reinforcement under the Duke of Lancaster was sent from England to Brittany, whence it marched overland to the south, and by December 1366 thirty thousand mounted troops were concentrated on the frontier of Navarre. It was by general consent admitted to be the finest army that had ever been seen in Europe; so rapid had been the growth of military efficiency in England under the two great Edwards. It was organised in the usual three divisions, the vanguard being under command of the Duke of Lancaster, with Sir John Chandos at his side. The battle was under the command of the Prince himself, and the rearguard under a Gascon noble and famous soldier, the Captal de Buch. Every man wore the red cross of St. George on a white surcoat and on his shield, a badge which henceforth became distinctive of the English soldier for two centuries. The Spaniards, it is worth noting, wore a scarf, a fashion which, already two generations old, was destined to last through our great Civil War, and to survive, in the form of a sash, to the present day.

On Monday the 22nd of February 1367 the first division crossed the Pyrenees by the Pass of Roncesvalles. The next two followed it on the two succeeding days, and the whole force was reunited at Pampeluna. The Prince had now two lines of operations open to him, both leading to his objective, Burgos; the one by Vittoria and Miranda on the Ebro, the other by Puente la Reyna and Logrono. He chose the former, the identical line followed in the contrary direction by Wellington in chase of the beaten French, and sent only a small detachment of volunteers under Sir Thomas Felton along the latter route. This party of Felton's deserves mention as the first body of English irregular cavalry under a reckless and daring officer. No exploit was too hare-brained for them and they did excellent service, for they were the first to find contact with the Spanish Army, at Navarete, and having obtained it they preserved it, keeping the prince admirably informed of the enemy's movements.

Henry of Trastamare, on learning the advance of the English, crossed the Ebro and marched on Vittoria, but finding that the Black Prince had been beforehand with him fell back on Miranda. Felton's volunteers stuck to him so persistently and impudently during this retreat that the Spaniards at last lost patience and attacked them in overwhelming force. The English, a mere hundred men, were too proud to retire but stood firm on the hill of Arinez, the very spot where Picton broke the French centre in the battle of the 21st of June 1813, and were killed to a man. Henry then recrossed the Ebro to his first posi-

BATTLE OF
POICTIERS
Sep.r 19th 1356

ENGLISH

FRENCH

One English Mile

tion at Navarete; the Black Prince crossed the same river at Logrono and on the 3rd of April the two hosts stood face to face on the plain between Navarete and Najera.

It is not easy to ascertain the force engaged on each side, but it is certain that the Black Prince, (April 3 1367), with about ten thousand men-at-arms and as many archers, was superior in numbers and very decidedly superior in the quality of his troops, Nevertheless the force had suffered much hardship, and the men were individually enfeebled by want of food. The Spanish Army was distributed into four divisions. The first of these, consisting of dismounted knights, was placed under the command of Bertrand du Guesclin and formed the first line.

The remaining three formed the second line; the largest of them, composed of mounted men-at-arms and a rabble of rude infantry, being drawn up in rear of the vanguard, while the other two, made up chiefly of light cavalry copied from the Moorish model, were drawn up on either flank slightly in advance of the second and in rear of the first line. The arrangement of the Black Prince's army was similar but more massive; first came the vanguard under John Chandos, then a second line with two flanking divisions pushed slightly forward, as in the Spanish Army, and lastly the third line in reserve. Every man in the English host was dismounted. The battlefield was a level plain; and the sight of the two armies advancing against each other, armour and pennons glancing under the morning sun was, in Froissart's words, great beauty to behold.

The English archers as usual opened the engagement, and then the divisions of Chandos and du Guesclin, the two most gallant and chivalrous soldiers of their day, met in full shock. In spite of a furious resistance the English, weakened by privation, were for a moment borne back. Chandos was overthrown and went near to lose his life. But meanwhile the English archers in the flanking divisions had driven off the light horse that stood before them, and now wheeling inward enveloped du Guesclin's devoted band on both flanks. The bastard Henry strove gallantly to save the day with the second line, but the Black Prince brought up not only a second line but a third, and the battle was soon over. Then the English men-at-arms flew, as at Poitiers, to their horses, and the defeat was turned into a rout. A rapid torrent, spanned by but a single bridge, barred the retreat of the fugitives; the narrow passage was choked by the press of the flying, and thousands were taken or slain.

This battle marks the zenith of early English military power. But the campaign was, after all, a failure. The ill faith of Pedro the Cruel forced the Black Prince to tax Gascony heavily for the expenses of the war; the province appealed to the King of France, and the prince was summoned to be judged before his peers at Paris as a rebellious vassal. He shook his head ominously when he received the message.

"We will go," he said, "but with helmet on head and sixty thousand men at our back."

The war with France broke out anew, and petty operations were soon afoot all over the country; but now noble after noble in Aquitaine and Gascony forsook his allegiance and revolted to the French. Disaster came thick upon disaster. The Earl of Pembroke, a new commander, disdaining the help of the veteran Chandos, was defeated, and Chandos himself, while advancing to his relief, was slain in a skirmish, to the grief alike of friend and of foe. The prince, already sickening of a mortal disease, turned in fury upon the insurgent town of Limoges, besieged it, took it, and ordered every soul in it to be put to the sword.

Three thousand men, women, and children were cut down, crying "Mercy, mercy!" but the stern man, too ill to ride, looked on unmoved from his litter, till at the sight of three French knights fighting gallantly against overwhelming odds his heart softened, and he gave the word for the slaughter to cease.

A few weeks later his little son, but six years old, the boy upon whom the great soldier had lavished all that was tender in his nature, died suddenly at Bordeaux. The blow aggravated the prince's sickness, and the physicians ordered him to England, in the faint hope that he might get better at home. He returned, hid himself in strict seclusion in his house at Berkhampstead, and waited for the end. Meanwhile things in France went from bad to worse. A great naval defeat before Rochelle cost England the command of the sea, and with the loss of the sea Guienne and Gascony were lost likewise. An expedition under John of Gaunt landed at Calais and marched indeed to Bordeaux, but lost four-fifths of its numbers through sickness on the way. By 1374 the English possessions in France were reduced to Calais, Bordeaux, and Bayonne; so swiftly had victory passed away with the withdrawal of the master's hand.

At length, in 1376, the prince came up to Westminster to attend, even in his sick-bed, the deliberations of Parliament. This was his last effort. Two months later, on the 8th of June, he summoned his faithful comrades to his chamber to bid them farewell, and as they filed past he thanked them for their good service and asked their pardon for that he could not reward them as he wished. Then he entreated them to be faithful to his son as they had been to himself: and they swore it, weeping like women, with all their hearts. The end came with a flash of the imperious soldier's spirit. Observing that a knight who had offended him had come in with the rest, the prince instantly bade him begone and see his face no more; and then the noble heart cracked, and with a last ejaculation that he forgave all men as he hoped to be forgiven, the Black Prince, the hope and pride and treasure of England, sank back and died.

Two months later he was buried with military pomp in the cathedral at Canterbury; and over his tomb were hung, and still hang, his helmet, his surcoat, his gauntlets, his crest, his shield, and his sword, (the sword is gone, but the scabbard remains), the veritable arms worn by the first great English soldier, (see details Dean Stanley's *Memorials of Canterbury*.) For a great soldier he was and a great commander. He could be stern and he could be merciless, but those were stern and merciless times, and the man whose last thoughts were for his comrades-in-arms was a chief who could hold men to him and a leader whom they would follow to the death. Men no longer pray for his soul in the chapel which he founded in the crypt of the cathedral; but morning and evening the voice of the trumpet, calling English soldiers to their work and dismissing them to their rest, peals forth from the barracks without and pierces faintly into the silence of the sanctuary, no unfitting requiem for the great warrior who, waiting for the sound of a louder trumpet, sleeps peacefully beneath the shadow of his shield.

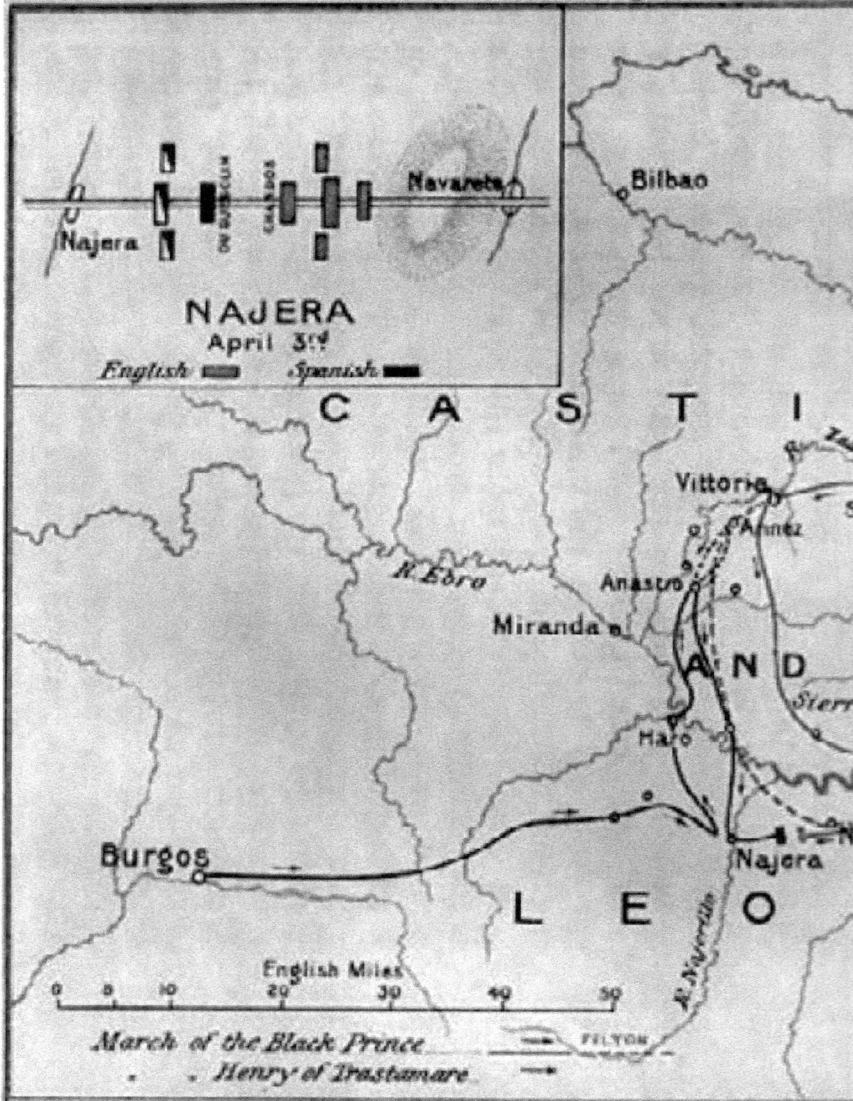

Najera

Navarete

Bilbao

NAJERA
April 3rd

English ▬▬▬ *Spanish* ▬▬▬

C A S T I

Vittoria

C'Annez

Anastro

R. Ebro

Miranda

A N D

Sterr

Haro

Burgos

Najera

L E O

English Miles

0   5   10   20   30   40   50

March of the Black Prince ——► FELTON

Henry of Trastamare ——►

R. Adour

Bayonne

St. Sebastian

GASCONY

St. Jean
Pied de Port

Roncevalles

LE

Sierra de Aratur

alvetierra

Sierra de Andea

Pampeluna

NAVARRE

PYRENEES

A

Puente la Reina

n de Cantabric

Logrono

avarete

N

R. Aragon

ARAGON

R. Ebro

Tudela

Chapter 4

Spread of English Tactics

The works of the Black Prince lived after him. Not that we must look for them immediately in England, where we now enter on forty years of intestine division and civil strife. We do indeed find that Richard the Second, on his invasion of Scotland in 1385, adopted for his army the organisation that had been taught by his father at Navarete; but we discover no trace of military progress. Far more instructive is it to look to the continent of Europe and watch the spread of English military ideas there. It has already been seen that the French, not daring to meet the English archers on horseback, adopted the English system of dismounting for action; and it is interesting to note that the same fashion spread to Germany and Italy, steadily tending to overthrow the supremacy of cavalry wrought by the feudal system, and to make a revolution in the art of war.

Not one of the nations, however, seems to have grasped the pith of the English tactics, the combination of the offensive and defensive elements in the infantry. The French indeed, under King Charles the Sixth, strove to raise up archers, and with all too good success, for they became so efficient that they were esteemed a menace to the nobility, and were soon effectively discouraged out of existence. Perhaps the most striking example of the misapplication of the English system is the conduct of the Austrian commander at Sempach, 1382, who by dismounting his knights deliberately gave away every advantage to the Swiss, and thus helped forward that nation on the way to make its infantry the model of Europe; a very significant matter in the history of the art of war.

But the truest disciples of the Black Prince were the English Free Companies, from whom there descended to England, and indeed to Europe, a legacy of a remarkable kind. These companies were military societies framed very much on the model of the ancient trade-guilds, and had as good a right to the name as they. A certain number of adventurers invested so much money in the creation of a trained body of fighting men, and took a higher or lower station of command therein, together with a larger or smaller share of the profits, according to the proportion of their venture.

If any man wished to realise his capital he could sell out, provided that he could find a buyer; if any one partner seemed to the rest to be undesirable they would buy him out and take in another. Thus grew up what was known as the purchase-system. The abuse of their monopoly by these companies drove the sovereigns of Europe after a time to issue commissions to their subjects to raise companies for their own service only; but even so the commercial basis of the company remained unchanged, being only widened when the time came for the amalgamation of companies into regiments. These military adventurers taught the nations the new art of war, and the nations could not but follow their model.

The greatest leader of free companies was an Englishman, a pupil of the Black Prince but greater even than his master, John Hawkwood. It is true that he did his work for foreign nations and in a foreign land, but even so his name must not be omitted from a history of the British Army. The company which he commanded, English almost to a man, was the terror of Italy, and not only the most formidable in the field but the smartest to the eye, for its arms were burnished till they shone like silver. Hawkwood, though a mercenary, was celebrated as the only one who never broke faith, and as a general his reputation was European. The action which he fought at Castagnaro, (1387), when, in spite of great inferiority in numbers, he deliberately laid his plans for a sudden counterstroke, after the manner of Poitiers, extorts the admiration even of modern generals. Still more remarkable is his once famous retreat in the face of an overwhelming force from the Adda to the Adige, (1391), and perhaps greatest of all was the closing scene of that retreat. For, as he lay encamped in the plains by the Adige, the enemy broke the dykes of the river and turned the whole flood of its waters upon his army.

It was night, and the men were encamping, weary after a hard day's march, when the deluge came upon them. Everything conspired to create a panic, but Hawkwood's coolness and confidence were equal to the danger. He bade every horseman take up one of the foot-men behind his saddle, and then placing himself at their head he led them through ten miles of the trackless waste of water, never less than girth-deep, and brought them out by sheer sagacity, not indeed without loss but without heavy loss, to the dry bed of the river. This was in his last campaign, when he was past seventy years of age; and Florence, the state which he had long faithfully served, voted him a pension for life and a monument even during his lifetime. He was making arrangements to return to England when he died; and King Richard the Second begged the city of Florence that the bones of so famous a warrior might be returned to his native land. The request was gracefully granted by the citizens, but the last resting-place of Hawkwood is now unknown. His monument in the cathedral at Florence records that he was the most skilful general of his age, a height of military fame that has been reached by one other Englishman only, John, Duke of Marlborough.

Yet another action must be briefly noticed to show the value set on English military skill. During the invasion of Portugal by the King of Castile, in 1385, the Portuguese were joined by a party of about five hundred English adventurers, whose leaders appear to have directed most of the operations. It was under their guidance that the decisive Battle of Aljubarotta, August 14, 1385, of which the Portuguese are still proud, was finally fought; and it is worthy of remark that, finding no advantageous position to hand, they deliberately constructed by means of abattis an imitation of the position of Poitiers, making it unassailable from the front except through a narrow strait, which was purposely left open and lined with archers.

Marvellous to relate, the Spaniards and the French, who were fighting with them, rushed straight into the trap, and were of course utterly overthrown; whereupon, in due accordance with precedent, the Portuguese made their counter-attack and won a complete victory. (Sir Arthur Wellesley occupied the Spanish position on his march to Roliça—*Conversations of the Duke of Wellington*). All this was due, as Froissart says, to the counsel of the English; and indeed, little though we may be conscious of it, it is doubtful whether even after Waterloo the prestige of English soldiers was greater than at the end of the fourteenth century.

But while the English military doctrines were thus spreading themselves over Europe, fresh innovations, which were destined to render them obsolete, were already making rapid progress. Artillery in the hands of the Germans was tending more and more to lose its cumbrous character and to take new form in mobile and practicable weapons. The heavy bombards, which could be neither elevated nor traversed, had before the close of the fourteenth century given place to lighter guns of smaller bore fixed on to the end of a shaft of wood and supported on a fork or hook, whence they derived their name of *Hakenbüchse*, a word soon corrupted by the English into hackbut, hagbush, and finally harquebus.

A later improvement had fitted guns with a stock like that of the cross-bow, which could be brought up to the shoulder, thus more readily aligning the barrel to the eye. The step from this to the hand-gun, which could be served out as the individual weapon of a single man, was but a short one and was soon to be taken. But as the traditions of Wellington and the Peninsula were to be tried once more at Alma and Inkerman before they finally perished, so the system of the two great Edwards was to be revived forty years after Navarrete at Agincourt.

It is unnecessary to dwell on the pretensions which were put forward to excuse the wanton aggression of Henry the Fifth against France, (1415). Ambitious, like Frederick the Great, of military glory he made his will the true ground for his action, counting on the spirit of a people that was never strongly averse from a French war. The military devices introduced by the Edwards, the commissions of array, (recognised by a statute of 5 Henry IV., the enactment relied on later by Charles I), and the system of indentures, were still in good working order, while the discipline of the Black Prince, like his order of battle, was stereotyped in a written code of Ordinances of War.

All the old machinery was therefore to hand; and perhaps the most noteworthy change that had come over the English military world was the doubling of the archers' wages from threepence to sixpence a day. Parliament voted the king a large sum of money, which however proved to be insufficient, for, significantly enough, not a contractor would furnish his contingent of men without security for the repayment of his expenses. The crown jewels were pledged in all directions, ships were hired in Holland and in England, seamen were impressed, artisans of every trade, from the miner to the farrier, were engaged, and on the 7th of August 1415 the army embarked at Southampton and the adjacent ports, and sailed for the Seine.

The whole fleet numbered some fourteen hundred vessels, and the army is reckoned at thirty thousand men, men-at-arms with their attendants, and archers both mounted and afoot, all distinguished by the red cross of St. George. Further, there was a great train of the newest and best artillery, great guns called by pet names such as the London and the King's Daughter, the whole under the charge of four German gunmasters.

On the second day out the fleet anchored before Harfleur. A day was taken up by the disembarkation, which was unhindered by the French; and by the 19th of August the town was fully invested. Then came a month of siege, wherein the art that was dying blended strangely with that which was just coming to birth; wooden towers and quaint engines that might have been employed by the Romans plying side by side with sap and mine and countermine and the latest patterns of German artillery. The French made a most gallant defence, and dysentery breaking out in the English camp swept off thousands of the besiegers; but at length the heavy guns prevailed. The garrison begged for terms, praying that the king would make his gunners to cease, "for the fire was to them intolerable." On the 22nd of September the capitulation was agreed on, and Harfleur received an English garrison. It was the first town that the English had reduced by the fire of cannon.

But Henry was not yet satisfied. Two-thirds of his force had melted away, dead or invalided, but he had no intention of re-embarking at Harfleur. He devoted a fortnight to the repair of the defences of the captured town, and then collecting provisions for eight days he marched northward for Calais with an army, or, as we should now call it, a flying column, of nine thousand men.

Meanwhile the French, disorganised though they were by the insanity of their king, Charles the Sixth, began to bestir themselves, and collecting an army of sixty thousand men, fourteen thousand of them men-at-arms and several thousand archers and cross-bowmen, determined to hold the line of the Somme and bar Henry's passage of the river. Henry's idea, dictated like the whole of his campaign by the precedent of Edward the Third, had been to cross the Somme by the ford of Blanche Tache. He now learned that the passage was defended by the French in force. He wheeled at once to the right, and following the left bank of the river upward, tried in vain to find a crossing-place. Every bridge was broken down and every ford beset. It was plain that he was more effectually entrapped even than his predecessor Edward.

The eight days' supply of provisions was now consumed, (October), and the position of the English became most critical. Retreat Henry would not, force the passage of the Somme he could not. He decided to follow the river upward to its headwaters, and on reaching Nesle learned from a countryman of a ford, the access to which lay across a morass. Two causeways that provided a footing over it had been broken down by the French, but these were quickly repaired with wood and faggots and straw till they were broad enough to admit three horsemen abreast. Henry himself was indefatigable in the work. He took personal charge of one end of the passages, and appointed special officers to attend to the other. The baggage was carried over along one causeway, and the men by the second. Thus the passage both of morass and river was accomplished between eight in the morning and an hour before dusk of an October day. The French, who were lying in force at Peronne, now for some unexplained reason retreated towards the north-west, but sent, according to custom, a challenge to Henry to fix time and place for battle.

"I am marching straight to Calais through open country," he replied. "You will have no difficulty in finding me." And he continued his advance.

At Peronne the English struck the Line of the French march and looked for an immediate engagement. The force moved in order of battle, every man armed and ready for action, while the archers by Henry's order carried a stake, eleven feet long and pointed at both ends, to make them defence against cavalry. To their surprise no enemy appeared; and Henry was presently able to disperse his force along a wider front, with the advantage alike of obtaining easier supply of victuals and surer information of the enemy. The English were much distressed by want of bread: other provisions were abundant, but grain was absolutely undiscoverable. Nevertheless discipline was most strictly enforced, and the order of the columns, as the speed of the march can avouch, was quite admirable. Robbery of churches or peasants, the slightest irregularity on the march or in the camp, the presence of women in the camp, all offences alike were visited with the severest punishment.

One man, whom Shakespeare has immortalised as Bardolph, was detected in the theft of a pyx: he was paraded through the army as a criminal and hanged. Even French writers admit that the English dealt more mercifully with them than their own countrymen. The king himself avoided anything that might seem to indicate the slightest discouragement. One night he missed the camping-ground assigned to his division and took up that of the vanguard. "God forbid that in full armour I should turn back," he said; and pushing the vanguard further forward, he halted for the night where he stood.

On the 24th of October, Henry, who was lying at Frevent on the River Canopes, was informed by his scouts that the French were moving forward from St. Pol and must inevitably get ahead of him. He pushed on to Blangy, crossed the River Ternoise there, and advancing to Maisoncelle drew up his army in battle order before it. The whole French Army was before him at Ruisseauville, but as dusk fell without an attack he withdrew for the night to Maisoncelle, and conscious of his desperate situation opened negotiations with the French, offering to restore Harfleur and make good all injuries if he might be permitted to evacuate France in peace. His overtures were rejected and he was warned to fight on the morrow. On the same evening the French moved down to a narrow plateau between the villages of Tramecourt and Agincourt, and there, cramped into a space far too narrow for sixty thousand men, they halted till the morrow within less than a mile of the English position.

The night was spent in very different fashion in the two camps. The French, doubtless much inconvenienced by the straitness of their quarters, were shouting everywhere for comrades and servants as noisily as a mob of sheep; while some, forgetting the lesson of Poitiers, gambled for the ransom of the prisoners that they were to take in the morrow's battle. Huge fires were kept burning round their banners, for the rain was incessant, and the English could see everything that passed among them. They too began shouting like the French till sternly checked by the king; and then the English camp fell silent, and the men, forbidden to forget their situation in the din of their own voices, sat down to face it in all its stern reality.

They could be excused if they felt some misgiving. They had covered over three hundred miles in a continuous march of seventeen days, often in hourly expectation of a fight; for four days they had not tasted bread; and now, after a few short hours more of waiting in the ceaseless pattering rain, they were to meet a host outnumbering them by five to one. Arms and bowstrings were overhauled and repaired; and the priests had little rest from the numbers that came to them for shrift. But in the discipline of that silence lay the promise of success.

At dawn of the next morning, October 25, Henry was astir, fully armed but bare-headed, riding a gray pony. Presently he led the army out of Maisoncelle to a newly-sown field, which was the position of his choice, and drew it up for battle. Every man was dismounted, and horses and baggage were parked in the rear under the protection o a small guard. But the numbers of his army were so weak that the favourite formation of the Black Prince could not be followed. The vanguard under the Duke of York became the right, the battle under the king the centre, and the rearguard under Lord Camoys the left of a single line, which even then was ranked but four men deep. It was a first example of English line against French column. Henry made the men a short speech, recalling to them the deeds of their fathers, and then the whole host kneeled down, thrice kissed the ground, and rose upright again into its ranks.

Meanwhile not a sign of attack came from the French. Their order of battle had been determined many days before, but it was ill adapted to so narrow a position. It was evident that only the vanguard could possibly come into action, and such was the indiscipline that every man of rank wished to command it. Finally the whole of the magnates were placed in the vanguard, and its strength was made up to about seven thousand men-at-arms, every one of them dismounted. On each flank was a wing of twelve hundred more dismounted men, and on their flanks again two small bodies of cavalry, three hundred on the right, and eight hundred on the left, which were designed to gallop down upon the archers. This was the first French line. The second was also made up of about eight thousand dismounted men-at-arms; while the remainder, who were ordered to dismount but would not, composed the third line. The whole stood on ploughed ground, soaked by the rain of the previous night and poached deep by the trampling of innumerable feet.

The French took advantage of the delay to give their men breakfast, an example which Henry immediately followed. Then seeing that the enemy remained motionless he prepared to attack. A gray old warrior, Sir Walter Erpingham, galloped forward with two *aides-de-camp* to make the necessary changes of formation. The archers were deployed in front and flanks, and when all was ready old Sir Walter tossed his baton into the air and sang out "Now strike." Then galloping back to the king's battalion he dismounted and took his place in the ranks.

The king, already dismounted, gave the word "Forward banner," and the English answered with a mighty cry, the forerunner of that "stern and appalling shout" which four centuries later was to strike hesitation into so fine a soldier even as Soult. Then the whole line advanced in close array, with frequent halts, for the ground was deep, and the archers in their leather jackets and hose, ragged, hatless, and shoeless after two months of hard work, could easily wear down the men-at-arms in their heavy mail. Artillery in such a sea of mud could not be brought into position on either side, and the German gunners took no part in the fight. The French on their side stood firm and closed up their ranks. They were so heavily weighted with their armour, always heavier than that of the English, that they could hardly move, and their front was so much crowded that they could not use their archers; so they broke off their lances as at Poitiers to the length of five feet, and stood in dense array, thirty-one ranks against the English four.

Arrived within range the archers struck their stakes slantwise into the ground, and drew bow. The French vanguard then shook itself up and advanced slowly, while the cavalry on their flanks moved forward against the archers. The division of three hundred lances on the right made but a poor attack; little more than half of them really came on, and even these their horses, maddened as at Crecy by the pain of the arrows, soon carried in headlong confusion to the rear. The stronger division on the left charged home, and the leader and one or two others actually reached the line of stakes; but the stakes had no firm hold in the mud; the horses tripped over them and fell, and not one rider ever rose again.

The remainder had as usual been carried back by their wounded horses upon their comrades in rear, and thence with them upon the wings of dismounted men-at-arms in which they tore terrible gaps. The centre of the French vanguard fared little better. Dazzled by the eastern sun that shone full in their eyes, and bending their heads before the sleet of arrows, they lost all idea of their direction, and became so clubbed together that they could not use their weapons. By sheer weight they forced back the English men-at-arms a lance's length, and for a time they fought hard.

King Henry was twice struck heavily on the helmet, one blow lopping a branch from the crown that encircled it. But meanwhile the archers had noted the gaps torn by the horses in the wings of the French fighting line. They dropped their bows, and with whatever weapon—axe, hammer, or sword—that hung at their girdle, they fell, light and active, upon the helpless, hampered men-at-arms and made fearful havoc of them. The French centre, exposed by the defeat of the wings to attack on both flanks, gave way before the king's battalion, and their first line was utterly defeated. There was no question of flight among the French men-at-arms, for the unhappy men could not move. The English simply took off the helmets of their prisoners, and, leaving them thus exposed, pressed on against the second line.

This, however, was already shaken by the defeat of the vanguard;

and though one leader who had arrived late in the field, the Duke of Brabant, set a gallant example, he was quickly cut down, and the defeat of the second line followed quickly on his fall. The third line still remained, but being mounted, contrary to orders, had no mind to stay and fight, but turned and fled, leaving some few of their leaders alone to redeem French honour by a hopeless struggle and a noble death.

This battle was hardly won when word was brought to Henry that his baggage, with all his treasure as well as all the horses, was in the hands of plunderers. The guard in fact had been unable to resist the temptation to join in the fight, and had left the baggage to take care of itself. The momentary confusion hereby caused gave some of the French time to rally, and Henry, not knowing how great the danger might be, ordered every man to kill his prisoners. The English hesitated, less possibly from humanity than from reluctance to lose good ransom, whereupon Henry told off two hundred archers for the duty, which was promptly carried out.

He can hardly be blamed, for the fight had been won less by the slaughter than by the capture of the men-at-arms; and the risk of undertaking a new attack in front with some thousands of unwounded prisoners in rear, was serious. Be that as it may, the deed was done. Henry then advanced against the rallied French and quickly broke them up; and at four o'clock, the victory being at last complete, he left the field. The French loss in nobles alone numbered from five to eight thousand men killed, exclusive of common men. A thousand prisoners and a hundred and twenty banners were taken. The losses of the English are uncertain, but probably did not exceed a few hundreds, the most distinguished of the fallen being the Duke York.

So ended the great fight which King Harry himself decreed to be called by the name of Agincourt, (more correctly Azincourt). It sums up in itself the leading features of Creçy, Poitiers, and Cocherel, in a word of all the finest actions of the Edwards. But it was, as fate ordained, but the afterglow of the glory of the Plantagenets, not the light of a sun new risen like a giant to run his course.

To attempt to follow the later campaigns of Henry the Fifth in France would be alike tedious and unprofitable. To the last he stuck to the principles of the Black Prince, but his military talents ripened year after year, and while he lived France trembled under his sword. Finally, torn to pieces by the strife of Burgundian and Armagnac, France by the Treaty of Troyes surrendered her kingship into his hand. The contempt of the English for their enemy was such that the men once assaulted and captured a town without orders. But in the very next year came a reverse that boded ominously for the future. The Duke of Clarence was defeated at Beaugé, less by the French than by a body of Scottish auxiliaries, who had been sent to their assistance under the Earl of Buchan. Henry had hoped that the Scots would not fight against him, and ordered them henceforth to be treated as rebels, but it was to no purpose. The reader should take note of this fateful year 1421, for it marks the permanent entrance of the Scots into the service of France, a fact full of import for both countries. Moreover, he will in due time see a regiment, still called the Royal Scots, withdrawn from the French Army to become the first of the English Line.

The return of King Henry to France after Beaugé soon re-established the ascendency of the English arms; and then, while still in the prime of life, he sickened even in the midst of his operations and died, (1422). He was but thirty-four years of age, a great administrator, a great captain, and above all a grand disciplinarian. Yet he was no brutal martinet; nay, when once he had cast his wild days behind him he never even swore. "Impossible," or "It must be done," was the most that he said. But:—

> He was so feared by his princes and captains that none dared to disobey his orders, however nearly related to him, and the principal cause was that if anyone transgressed his orders he punished him at once without favour or mercy.—Monstrelet.

He and the army that fought with him at Agincourt are the true precursors of Craufurd and the Light Division. His body, borne with mournful pomp from the castle of Vincennes, still rests among us in Westminster Abbey, and above it still hang his saddle, his shield blazoned with the lilies of France, and the helmet, deeply dinted by two sword-cuts, which he wore at Agincourt. Not for three centuries was another soldier to rise up in England of equal fame with the Black Prince, John Hawkwood, and King Harry the Fifth.

CHAPTER 5

Continuation of the War under the Duke of Bedford

It is now our sad duty to watch the military glory of the Planta-genets wane fainter and fainter, until it disappears, to be followed by a period of darkness until the light is slowly rekindled at the flame of foreign fires. The decline of our supremacy in arms was not at first rapid. John, Duke of Bedford, possessed a combination of military and administrative talent little less remarkable than that of his brother the late King, and as Regent of France he took up the reins of govern-ment and command with no unskilful hand. Everything turned upon the maintenance of existing factions in France.

England working with Burgundy, the red cross of St. Andrew with the red cross of St. George, could preserve the English dominion; otherwise that dominion must inevitably fall. The French, after the lull created by Henry's death, gathered an army together of which the kernel was three thousand Scots, and marched into Burgundy to be-siege Crevant. A body of four thousand picked English and Burgun-dians at once hastened after them, and although outnumbered, and compelled, by the advance of a second French army in their rear, to fight their battle and win it at whatever cost, they defeated the enemy completely and cut the Scots to pieces almost to a man. All was still done as King Harry had done it. English tactics were forced, on pain of death, upon English and Burgundians alike, and discipline was most strictly preserved.

★★★★★★

See Philippe de Commines, bk. i. chap. iii. "(At the Battle of Montlhéry, 1464) the most honourable persons fought on foot among the archers ... which order they learned of the English, who are the best shot in the world."

******

It was not a promising beginning for the French, but Scotland was ready to furnish more men, and France not less ready to receive them; and so the extraordinary struggle of French against French, and English against Scots was renewed once more.

Early in 1424 ten thousand Scottish men-at-arms, under Archibald, Earl of Douglas, arrived at Rochelle, and were welcomed with eagerness by the French. Douglas was created Duke of Touraine, and all went merrily until on the 17th of August French and English, with their allies, met under the walls of Verneuil. The French and Scots numbered close on twenty thousand men, the English twelve thousand, of whom eight thousand were archers. Contrary to the hitherto accepted practice, the French formed their army into a single huge central battalion of dismounted men, with cavalry on each wing, the mounted men being designed to fall upon the English flanks and rear. Bedford, who commanded the English, imitated the enemy in forming only a single battalion, but dismounted the whole of his force, covering his front and flanks with archers, who as at Agincourt carried stakes as a defence against the attack of horse. His baggage he parked in rear, the horses being tied collar to tail that they might be the less easily driven off; and he appointed as baggage-guard no fewer than ten thousand archers.

For the whole morning the two armies stood opposite to each other in order of battle, each waiting for the other to attack; but at last, at three in the afternoon, the French advanced and were received by the English with a mighty shout. The French cavalry on the wings charged, broke through the archers, and sweeping round the English rear fell upon the baggage. They were greeted by the guard with a shower of arrows, but contrived none the less to carry off some quantity of spoil, with which they galloped away, feeling sure that the day was won, (observe how early cavalry fell into the fault which caused the loss of Naseby).

But meanwhile the two battalions of dismounted men-at-arms, those on the French side being exclusively Scots, had closed and were fighting desperately. For a moment the English were beaten back by superior numbers; but Salisbury, John Talbot, and other tried leaders were with them, and they soon recovered themselves. The archers on the wings rallied to their aid, while those of the baggage-guard, freed from all further alarm of cavalry, hurried up with loud shouts in support. The Scots wavered, and the English pressing forward with one supreme effort broke through their ranks, split up the battalion, and threw the whole into helpless confusion. And then began a terrible carnage, for the Scots had told Bedford that they would neither give nor receive quarter, and they certainly received none. Five thousand men, mostly Scots, were killed on the French side, John Stewart, Earl of Buchan, the Earl of Douglas and James his son being among the slain, and two hundred more were taken prisoners. Of the English some sixteen hundred only went down.

To France Verneuil was a disaster little less crushing than Agincourt, and indeed it seemed as though she had passed irrevocably under English dominion. All was however spoiled by Bedford's brother Humphrey, Duke of Gloucester, who, having made a match with a rich heiress, Jacqueline of Holland, carried away English troops to take possession of her dower-lands, and, worst of all, gave the deepest offence to Burgundy. At home Humphrey was equally troublesome, so much so that in 1425 Bedford was compelled to return to England to set matters right. It was not until three years later, 1428, that he took the field again, well reinforced with men and with a powerful train of artillery. So far we have rarely found artillery employed except for sieges, but henceforth we see gunners regularly employed at the high wage of a man-at-arms, one shilling a day, and "hand-cannons" and "little cannons with stone shot of two pounds weight," playing ever a more prominent part in the field.

Against his better judgment Bedford now resolved to carry the war across the Loire, and detached the Earl of Salisbury with ten thousand men to the siege of Orleans. The operations opened unfortunately with the death of Salisbury, who was mortally wounded by a cannon-shot while examining the enemy's works; but the investment was carried on with spirit by the Earl of Suffolk, and a little action at the opening of 1429 showed that the English superiority still held good. This, the Battle of Roveray, better known as the action of the Herrings, has a peculiar interest, though the occasion was simple enough. Lent was approaching; and as, among the many complications of mediaeval warfare, the observance of the fast was by no means forgiven to fighting men, it was necessary to send provisions of "Lenten stuff," principally herrings, to the besieging force round Orleans.

★★★★★★

The same difficulty of a Lenten campaign cropped up at the siege of Orleans a century later. It was surmounted by the

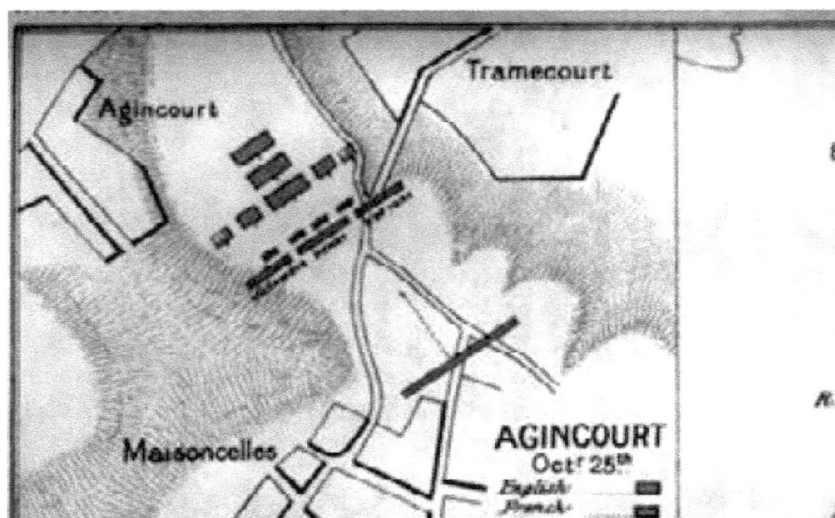

AGINCOURT
Octr 25th

English
French

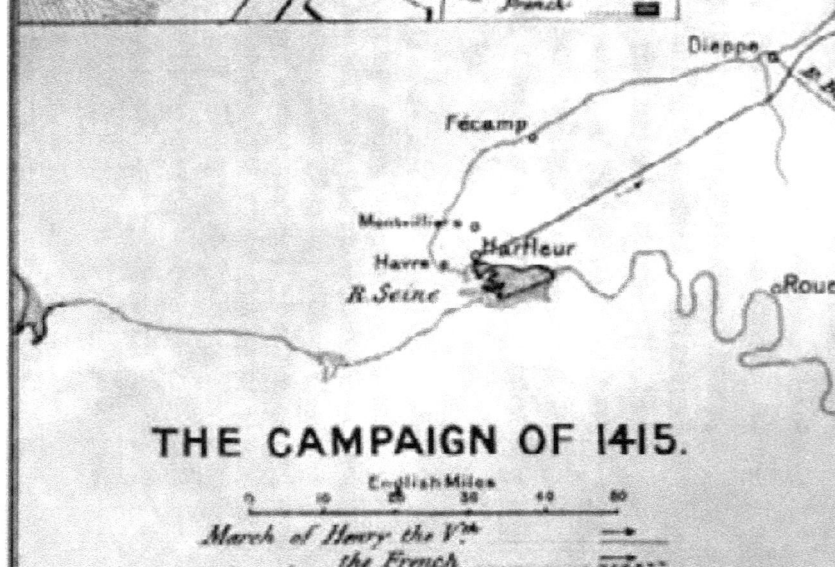

THE CAMPAIGN OF 1415.

English Miles

March of Henry the Vth
the French

general's insisting that the papal legate, who was in the camp, should grant a dispensation, which he very unwillingly did; whereupon every man in the army *'pria Dieu fort pour M. le legat'*—Brantôme, ed. Elzev. vol. i.

★★★★★★

The convoy being large was provided with an escort of sixteen hundred men under command of Sir John Falstolfe. The French and Scots decided to attack it on the march, but unfortunately could not agree as to their plan; the Scots insisting that it was best to dismount, the French preferring to remain in the saddle. Meanwhile Falstolfe with great dexterity drew his waggons into a leaguer, leaving but two narrow entrances defended by archers. It was the trap of Poitiers once more. The French and Scots after long discussion agreed to differ, and attacked each in their own fashion. The English archers shot with admirable precision; the Scots lost very heavily, the French after a short experience of the arrows rode out of range, and Falstolfe led his herrings triumphantly into Orleans, having killed close on six hundred of the enemy with trifling loss to himself. This was the last signal employment of the tactics of Poitiers, the last brilliant success of the English in the Hundred Years' War, the first glimpse of a lesson learnt by England from the military genius of a foreign power. For the tactics of the waggon were those of John Zizka, the greatest soldier of Europe in the fifteenth century.

From this point the story is one of almost unbroken failure for the English in France. They were now about to pass through the experience which later befell the Spaniards in the Low Countries, and the French themselves in the Peninsula. The turning-point is of course the appearance in the field of Joan of Arc, a phenomenon so extraordinary that it has become the exclusive property of the votaries of poetry and sentiment, and is, perhaps rightly, not to be rescued from their hands. It is certain that her military talents were of the slightest; but, on the other hand, she possessed the magic of leadership and the amazing power of restoring the moral strength of her countrymen, which had been impaired as never before by an endless succession of defeats.

The English not unnaturally attributed this power to witchcraft: for by what other agency could a peasant girl have checked the ever-victorious army? and the punishment of witchcraft being the fire they burnt her to death. Any other nation would have done the same in their place then, and there are still a few folks both in France and the United Kingdom who would do so now. But the fire in the marketplace of Rouen availed the English little. "The French," as Monstrelet says, believed that "God was against the English"; and the English began to believe it themselves.

For the woman's quick instinct and the pure insight of a saintly soul had guided the maid aright. The moral quality of the English force was corrupted, and needed only to meet some loftier spirit to fall into decay. The chivalrous character of the war was gone. Hostile commanders no longer laid each other friendly wagers on the success of their next operations. The army too was ceasing to be national; the English element was growing smaller and smaller in number, and fast sinking to the level of the lawless adventurers who furnished the majority in the ranks. Long contempt of the enemy had bred insolence and carelessness, and the old discipline was almost gone. The sight of a deer or a hare sufficed to set a whole division hallooing, sometimes, as at Patay, (1430), with disastrous results. On that day the French scouts, who were feeling for the enemy, roused a stag, which ran towards the English array, and was greeted with such a storm of yells as told the French all that they wanted to know.

The English force blundered on, without advanced parties of any kind, till it suddenly found itself on the verge of an engagement. Then the leaders wrangled as to the question of fighting in enclosed or open country, and, having finally in overweening confidence selected the open, were surprised and routed before the archers could plant their stakes in the ground. Worst of all, an officer in high command, Sir John Falstolfe, seeing that defeat was certain, disobeyed the order to dismount and galloped away. He was disgraced by Bedford, but was afterwards for some reason reinstated, though had Harry been king he would assuredly have lost his head. (He remains gibbeted, however, in the pages of Shakespeare, which is perhaps the worst fate that could have befallen him).

Among the French the revival of the military spirit soon showed itself in a remarkable development of new ideas. They had long copied, though with a bad grace, the English practice of dismounting men-at-arms and furnishing archers with a palisade of stakes, but in 1434 at Gerberoy they used the three arms, cavalry, infantry, and artillery, in combination, with signal success. Artillery was still so far a novelty in the field that only three years before, Sandacourt 1431, a whole army collected by the Duke of Bar, had flung itself howling to the ground at the first discharge; but the English archers, though they knew better than to behave thus, were sadly dismayed when the round stone shot came bounding within their trusted palisade. It was just after this, too, that two fatal blows were struck at the English by the shifting of Burgundy to the French side, and by the death of their ablest leader, John, Duke of Bedford.

Still the war, wantonly and foolishly continued by an inefficient government, dragged on and on, and, though not unbroken by occasional brilliant exploits, turned steadily against the English. The behaviour of the soldiers was sullied more and more by shameful barbarity; and gradually but surely their hold on Normandy and Guienne slipped from them. Truce was made at last in 1444, and Charles the Seventh seized the opportunity to execute a series of long-meditated reforms in the French Army. He established a national militia of fifteen companies of men-at-arms and archers, each six hundred strong, organised garrisons of trained men for the towns, took the greatest pains for the equipment, discipline, and regular payment of the troops, and formed the finest park of artillery thitherto seen.

In a word, he laid the foundation of the French standing army, with the Scottish archers and Scottish men-at-arms at its head, two famous corps that remained in their old place on the army-list until the French Revolution. Thus French military organisation, spurred by a century of misfortune, made one gigantic bound ahead of English, and may be said to have kept the lead ever since.

In England there had been no such improvement. A feeble effort had been made to check by statute fraudulent enlistment, (1440), and the still graver abuse of embezzlement of the soldiers' pay by the captains, but this was of little help when the enforcement of the Act (18 Henry VI. cap. 18), was entrusted to so corrupt and avaricious a commander as the Duke of Somerset. Throughout the truce the soldiers on the English side behaved abominably; but, since they were robbed of their wages by their officers, it is hardly surprising that they should have repaid themselves by the plunder of the country. When finally the truce was broken, (1449), and the French invaded Normandy, the English dominion fell before them like a house of cards. Town after town, their garrisons depleted to fill Somerset's pocket, surrendered to superior force, and the English as they marched forth had the mortification to see the Normans gleefully doff the red cross of St. George for the white cross of France.

An attempt to save the province was foiled by the rout of the English reinforcements at Formigny, and Normandy, April 1450, was lost. Anjou and Maine had been already made over to the father of Henry the Sixth's Queen, and Guienne and Gascony, which had been English since the reign of Henry the Second, alone remained. Next year they too went the way of Normandy and were lost.

Gascony, however, notwithstanding her hot southern blood, was in no such anxiety as Normandy to be quit of the English, and sent messages to England that, if an army were sent to help her, she would revolt against the French to rejoin her old mistress. England lent a willing ear, and John Talbot, the veteran Earl of Shrewsbury, was sent out to this, his last campaign. The decisive battle, July 20 1453, was fought under the walls of Chatillon. The French were strongly entrenched, with three hundred pieces of artillery in position, a striking testimony to their military progress. The English fought with the weapon which for a century had won them their victories, and for the last as for the first battle of the Hundred Years' War, every man alighted from his horse.

John Talbot alone, in virtue of his fourscore years, remained mounted on his hackney; and with the indomitable old man at their head the English hurled themselves upon the entrenchment. It was a mad, desperate, hopeless venture, but they stormed forward with such impetuosity that they went near to carry the position. For a full hour they persisted, until at last, riddled through and through by the fire of the artillery, they fell back. Then the French sallied forth and turned the defeat into a rout. Old John Talbot's pony was shot under him, and being pinned to the ground under the dead animal he was killed where he lay.

Young John Talbot, Lord Lisle, refused to leave his father, and fell by his side. The army was dispersed over Aquitaine, and the ancestral domains of seven generations of English kings passed from them for ever. By the irony of fate a Scottish soldier, (Robert Patillock), was appointed to hold for the crown of France the French provinces that had clung with such attachment to England. Of all the great possessions of the English in France Calais now alone was left, to break in due time the heart of an English Queen.

At home the discontent over the national disgrace was profound. The people of course cast about to find a scapegoat, and after one or two changes finally fixed upon the blameless and unfortunate Henry the Sixth. Want of a strong central government was undoubtedly the disease from which England had suffered ever since the death of King Henry the Fifth, but for this the nation itself was principally responsible. It had chosen for its rulers the House of Lancaster because Henry of Bolingbroke had agreed to accept constitutional checks on the royal power before the country was ripe for self-government. It had thrown off the yoke of discipline which alone could enable it to tug the heavy load of English weal and English honour, and it paid the inevitable penalty. Numbers of republics have made the same mistake during the 19th century and have suffered or are suffering the same punishment. There is no surer sign of an undisciplined nation than civil war.

In the England of the fifteenth century the disease had been deeply aggravated by the interminable campaigns in France. All classes at home, from the highest to the lowest, were equally selfish and apathetic in respect of the national good: internal order was at an end, and riots and outrages which amounted to private war continued unceasingly and remained unrepressed. The system of indentures between king and subject for the supply of troops had been extended from subject to retainer and, as has been well said, the clause "for the King's service" could easily be dropped out of the contract, (Oman's *Warwick*). The red cross of St. George never appears in the English battlefields; red rose and white were indeed the emblems of contending factions, but we hear far more of the badges of great families, the ragged staff, the cresset and the like, and of the liveries, which, though forbidden by statute to any but the king, were conspicuous all through the Civil War.

The loss of France furnished but too much material to the hands of violence and strife. England was full of unemployed soldiers, who had been trained in the undisciplined school of French faction to treachery and plunder and all that is lowest and most inhuman in war. Hundreds of men who had held comfortable posts in French garrisons, and had turned them to purposes of brigandage, were cast adrift upon England, barbarised, brutalised, demoralised, to recoup themselves in their own country. After the peace of Brétigny the disbanded soldiery had made France their chamber and swept down thence upon Italy; the like men were now to be let loose upon England, and France was to be well avenged of her old enemy. (Yet they were not all ruffians, in the *Paston Letters* some professional soldiers hired for private defence are described as gentlemanly comfortable fellows, and their employer is warned that they must not be put to sleep more than two in a bed). Worst of all, the leaders of factions, in the madness of their animosity, were not ashamed to import foreign troops and set them at each other's throats.

I shall not dwell upon this miserable and disastrous period, marking as it does the wreck of our ancient military greatness. Such few military points as present themselves in the scanty chronicles of this time must be noted, and no more. Of the principal figures one only is to be remarked. Warwick the "King-maker" must be passed over as rather a statesman than a soldier; Margaret of Anjou—the pestilent, indomitable woman—must be remembered only for her importation of mercenaries; Edward the Fourth, full of the military genius of the Plantagenets, alone is deserving of lengthier mention. There was not an action at which he was present wherein he did not make that presence felt. It was he who at Northampton, (1460), turned his treacherous admission to the left of the Lancastrian position to instant and decisive account. It was he who in the following year, still only a boy of twenty, crushed Owen Tudor at Mortimer's Cross; it was he who held supreme command at that more terrible Marston Moor of the fifteenth century, the Battle of Towton.

This action has a peculiar interest as an example of English tactics and tenacity turned upon themselves.

The Lancastrians, sixty thousand strong, were formed up on a plateau eight miles to the north of Ferrybridge, March 28 1461, facing south—their right resting on a brook, called the Cock, their left on the Great North Road. It was a strong position, but too much cramped for their numbers, having a front of less than a mile in extent. They were probably drawn up according to the old fashion in three lines of great depth. The Yorkists numbered but five-and-thirty thousand, but they were expecting an additional thirteen thousand under the Duke of Norfolk, which, advancing from Ferrybridge, would come up on their own right and against the left flank of the enemy.

Edward appears to have remedied his numerical inferiority after the pattern of his great ancestor at Creçy by forming his army in echelon of three lines, refusing his right. The foremost or left line of the echelon was commanded by Lord Falconbridge, the second by Warwick, and the third by Edward in person. The Yorkists advancing northward to the attack had just caught sight of the enemy on a height beyond a slight dip in the ground called Towton Dale, when there came on a blinding snowstorm, which so effectually veiled both armies that it was only by their shouts that they could know each other's position. Falconbridge with great readiness seized the moment to push forward his archers to the edge of the plateau, whence he bade them shoot flight-arrows, specially adapted to fly over a long range, into the Lancastrian columns. This done he quickly withdrew

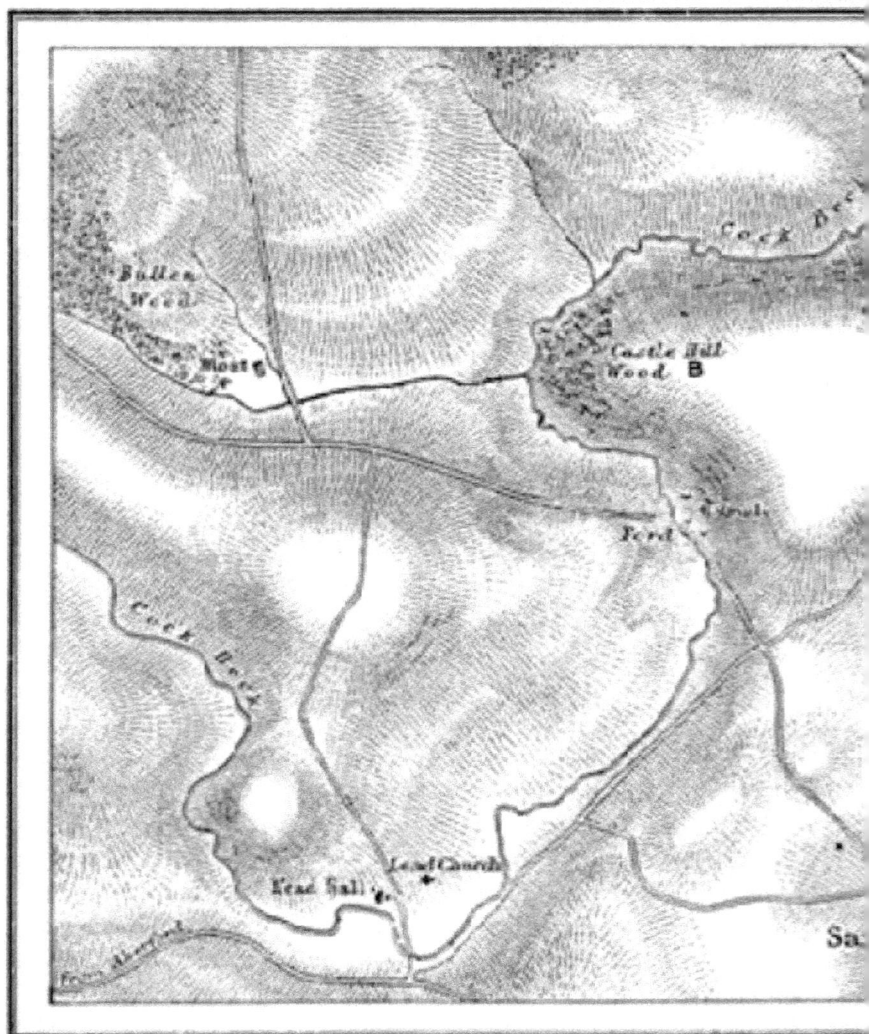

Lancastrian troops ▬▬▬   Yorkist troops ▬▬▬

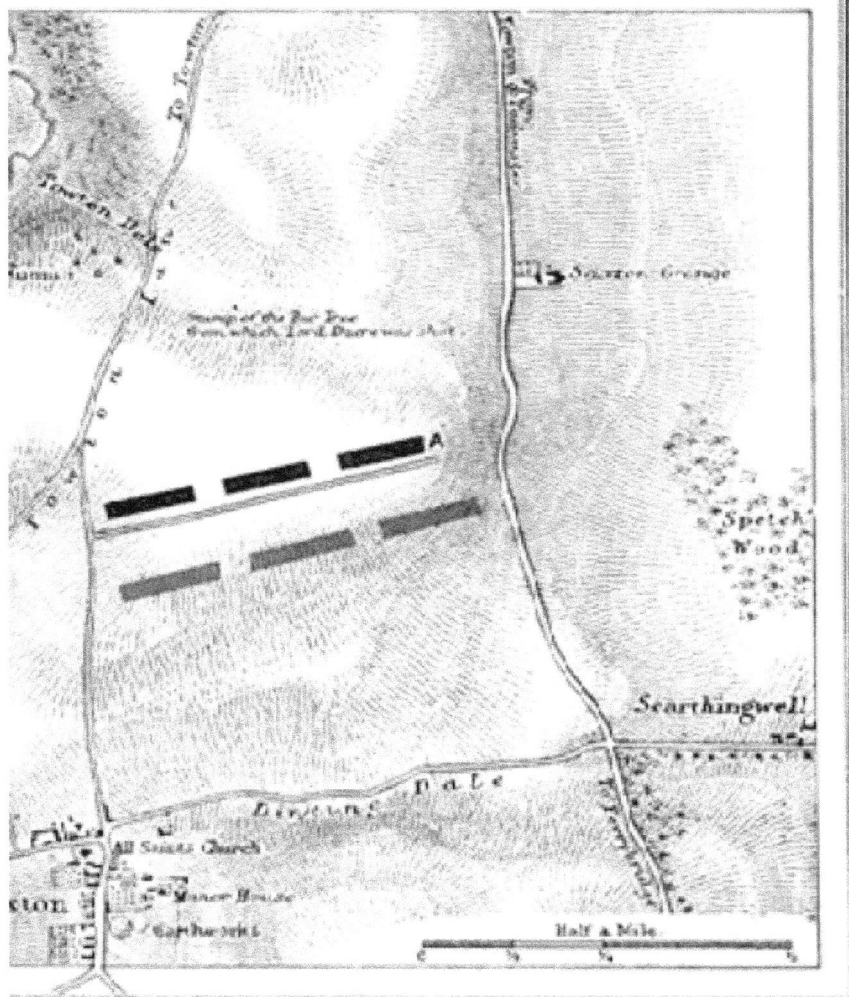

his men.

The Lancastrians thereupon poured in a tremendous shower of fighting arrows, all of which fell short of their supposed mark, and maintained it till their sheaves were well-nigh exhausted. Then Falconbridge again advanced and began to shoot in earnest; his men had not only their own stock of shafts but also those discharged by the enemy. The rain of missiles was too much for the Lancastrians: they broke from their position on the height and poured down across the dip to drive the Yorkists from the slope above it. Then the action became general and the whole line was soon hotly engaged.

What followed for the next few hours in the driving snow no one has told us, or, it is probable, could ever have told us. All that is certain is that the Lancastrians, though occasionally they could force the Yorkists back for a space, could never gain any permanent advantage, a fact that points to extremely judicious handling of the refused division by Edward. From five in the morning until noon the combat raged with unabated fury, and the pile of the dead rose so high that the living could hardly come to close quarters. At length at noon the Duke of Norfolk's column, timely as Blucher's, appeared in the Great North Road on the left flank of the Lancastrians, and began to roll them back from their position and from the line of their retreat.

Slowly and sullenly the Lancastrians gave way; there was probably little attempt to alter their disposition to meet the attack in their flank; but for three long hours more they fought, disputing every inch of ground, till at last they were forced back from it upon the swollen waters of the Cock. Then the rout and the slaughter became general; thousands were drowned in the brook; and the pursuit, wherein we again see the hand of Edward, was carried to the very gates of York. Thirty-five thousand Lancastrians and eight thousand Yorkists perished in the fight, an appalling slaughter for so miserable a cause. But this was a contest not merely of faction against faction, but of North against South; and the North never spoke disrespectfully of the South again. This perhaps was the principal result of what must be reckoned the most terrible battle ever fought by the English.

The decisive Battle of Barnet, April 14 1471, furnishes a still more brilliant instance of Edward's skill, and of his quickness to seize the vital point in a campaign. All turned upon his forcing his enemies to action before they could gather their full strength about them. Edward marched his men up to Warwick's position actually after dusk had fallen, a rare accomplishment in those days, and drew up his men as best

BATTLE OF TOWTON

he could in the dark. When day broke with dense fog he discovered that his army far out-flanked Warwick's left, and was as far out-flanked by Warwick's on his own left. The result seems to have been that the two armies edged continually round each other until their respective positions were reversed, for some of Warwick's cavalry, coming back from the pursuit of Edward's left, found itself on its return not, as it supposed, in rear of Edward's army, but of its own.

The cry of treason, always common in the Wars of the Roses, was quickly raised, and in the general confusion the battle was lost to Warwick. None the less the victory was due to Edward's promptness; and indeed the rapidity alike of his decisions and of his marches stamp him as a soldier of no ordinary talent, and as in many respects far in advance of his time.

For the rest the Wars of the Roses show unmistakable signs of the changes that were coming over the art of war.

★★★★★★

Allusion has already been made to the supplanting of the sheriff's authority by the barons in raising troops, and the consequent fashion of issuing liveries to the corps so formed. It is perhaps worth while to note and dismiss the minute point that the garrison of Calais, the only truly national force belonging at that moment to England, was clothed in scarlet jackets, and were the first English soldiers thus distinguished.

★★★★★★

A most important point is the ever increasing employment of artillery in the field and the greater value attached to it. Richard, Duke of York, is said to have had a great train of ordnance and so many as three thousand gunners with him at Dartmouth in 1452. Artillerymen were becoming far more common, and as a natural consequence bade fair to command a smaller price in the wage-market. From this time also it may be said that the duel of artillery tends to become the regular preliminary to a general action. Still more significant is the augmented prominence of the common foot-soldier, known from his peculiar weapon as the bill-man, who now begins to supplant the dismounted man-at-arms in the work of infantry, and as a natural consequence restores the latter to his proper station among the cavalry.

New weapons again make their appearance in the hands of the foot-soldier. Both Edward and Warwick introduced hired bands of Burgundian hand-gun men, whereby the English became acquainted with the new arm that was to drive out the famous bow. Again, on the field of Stoke, (1487), there were seen two thousand tall Germans armed with halberd and pike, under the command of one Martin Schwartz, who fought on the losing side, but stood in their ranks till they were cut down to a man.

★★★★★★

Readers of Kenilworth will remember the ballad quoted by Giles Gosling—

He was the flower of Stoke's red field
Where Martin Swart on ground lay slain.

★★★★★★

Lastly, the old order of battle in three lines was becoming rapidly obsolete. At Bosworth both armies were drawn up in a single line, with the cavalry on the wings; and the cavalry itself was beginning at the same time to forsake the formation in column for that in line, or as it was called, *en haye*.

All these changes were symptoms of a great movement that was passing over all Europe. The art of war, like all the other arts, was undergoing a transformation so fundamental that it has received the name of a renascence. England, cut off by her expulsion out of France from her former contact with continental nations, exhausted by her civil wars, reduced to her true position as a naval power, and above all wedded to the peculiar system which had brought her such success, lagged behind other nations in the path of military reform. The century of the Tudors' reign is for the English Army a century of learning, and to understand it aright we must first look abroad to the countries that were before her in the school, and glance at the innovations that were introduced by each of them in the course of the fifteenth and sixteenth centuries. Not without such study can we trace to their source innumerable points, great and small, that are observable in our army of today, nor grasp to the full the greatness of the English soldiers who, long before the renascence of the art of war, had divined its leading principles, had established for their country noble military traditions, and above all had made it a national principle that the English must always beat the French.

PLAN of the BATTLE
of
BOSWORTH,
and of the
Neighbourhood.

June 17 1789.
J Paddam del

Nether
Coton

St W Stanley's
Camp

King

Shenton

Dibbll

C King Richard's
DeWill

Henry's
Camp

Ambien Wood

Henry's

M Bate River

Radm
Plain
P

Tapid R

Dadlingto

Crown Hill
N

Stoke
Golding

Market Bosworth

Bull in the Oak

Cadeby

Duke of Norfolk's Camp

Sutton Heath

Sutton Field

Sutton Cheynell

Hall

Richard's Army

Stapleton

K.Richard's Camp

M

Lord Stanley's Camp

Scale ½ Mile

CHAPTER 6

Renaissance of the Art of War in Europe

Five years after the Battle of Agincourt, 1420, the religious wars in Bohemia had given birth to one of the great soldiers of the world's history, John Zizka, the blind general of the Hussites. His military genius, quickened by fanaticism and spurred by the stern necessity of encountering an enemy always superior in numbers and equipment, had led him to ideas which were far in advance of his age. A master in organisation and discipline, he had evolved literally out of nothing the most famous army of its day in Europe, and by inexhaustible activity and resource had rendered it invincible. Beginning with such rude material of war as waggons and flails, and with no more skilful men than poor Bohemian peasants, he matured a system of tactics which defeated not only the chivalry of Europe but even the light irregular cavalry, soon to become famous as hussars, of Hungary.

As victory supplied him with the means of procuring better arms, he rose rapidly to the occasion. Throwing all military pedantry to the winds he fought as his own genius dictated, and in the rapidity of his movements and unrelenting swiftness with which he followed up a victory he bears comparison with Napoleon. He was the first man to make artillery a manoeuvrable arm, the first to execute complicated evolutions in the face of an enemy, and the first to handle cavalry, infantry, and artillery in efficient tactical combination. The employment of waggons for defence we have already seen copied by the English at the Battle of the Herrings, but Zizka's influence, (he has left us two words, howitzer and pistol, both of which are derived from the Czech), spread far wider than this by breaking down the strength of European chivalry, and showing that drill, discipline, and mobility could make the poorest peasant more than a match for the armoured knight.

Zizka, however, had not been the first to deal a blow at the supremacy of feudal cavalry. The English archers and dismounted men-at-arms had been before him, and another power, which was destined to abolish that supremacy for ever, had been in some respects the predecessor even of the English. Allusion has already been made to the victory of the Swiss over the Austrian chivalry at Sempach, (1382); from that day it may be said that they began their advance to the highest military reputation of Europe. Appointed from the ruggedness of their country as well as by their own poverty to fight rather on their own feet than on horseback, cut off in great measure by the same causes from the feudalism that had overrun the rest of Europe, they were by nature destined to be infantry, and as infantry they developed their fighting system.

Beginning like all primitive footmen in all countries with the simple weapons of shield, spear, and axe, they improved upon them to meet their own peculiar wants. The problem before them was, how to defeat mounted men mailed from head to foot in the open field, how to keep the horses at a distance and cut through the iron shells that protected the men. The instinct of a Teutonic nation led them to give first attention to the cutting weapon. The English had turned their axes into broad-bladed bills; the Flemings had gone further and produced the *godendag*, a weapon good alike for cut and thrust; the Swiss, improving upon the *godendag*, invented the halberd, which combined a hook for pulling men out of the saddle, a point to thrust between the joints of their armour, and a broad heavy blade, the whole being set on the head of an eight-foot shaft. The weight of the halberd made it, as an old chronicler , (John of Winterthur) says, a terrific weapon, "cleaving men asunder like a wedge and cutting them into small pieces." (If the reader has ever plied a long billhook to cut down overhanging branches he will appreciate the power of the halberd). Altogether it was calculated to surprise galloping gentlemen who thought themselves invulnerable in their armour.

But the halberd did not solve the problem of keeping horses at a distance. For this purpose the primitive spear was lengthened more and more till it finally issued in the long pike, the pike of the eighteen-foot shaft, which for nearly two centuries ruled the battlefields of Europe. The birthplace of the long pike is obscure, but it was undoubtedly first brought into prominence by the Swiss, and that by a series of brilliant actions.

★★★★★★

The earliest mention of the long pike occurs in an order addressed to the burghers of Turin by Count Philip of Savoy in 1327; but whether Swiss borrowed it from Savoyards or Savoyards from Swiss is uncertain—(*Köhler*).

★★★★★★

Arbedo, 1422, attested the firmness of the new infantry in the. field; St. Jacob-en-Birs, 1444, where the Swiss detached. sixteen hundred men to fight against fifty thousand, its boundless confidence; and finally the three crushing defeats of Charles the Bold at Granson, Morat, 1476, and Nancy, 1477, established its reputation as invincible. For action the Swiss were generally formed in three bodies, van, battle, and rear—the van and rear being each of half the strength of the battle or main body. These bodies were always of a very deep formation, and if not actually square were very solidly oblong. Occasionally the whole were massed into one gigantic battalion in order that the proportion of pikes to halberds, which was about one to three, might go further in securing immunity from the attack of cavalry. The van, from the desperate nature of its work, was called the *Verlorener Hauf*, from which is derived our own term, not yet wholly extinct, forlorn hope.

★★★★★★

Compare the French equivalent, *enfans perdus*. *Hauf* was the regular German word for any mass of soldiers, from a company to a battalion. The English word *hope* therefore is a corruption, *hauf* having more to do with heap than hope.

★★★★★★

As regards discipline the Swiss appear to have been orderly and sober men until spoiled by the multitude of their successes, but at the last they became intolerably insubordinate. The cantons indeed were so deeply bitten with the military mania, that all great occasions, feasts, fairs, and even weddings, were made the occasion of some form of military display, while the very children turned out with drums, flags, and pikes, and marched with all the order and regularity of full-grown soldiers. In fact fighting became the regular trade of Switzerland, and as her people enjoyed for a time a practical monopoly of that trade they soon became grasping and avaricious, and would dictate to generals under threat of mutiny when and where they should fight, select their own position in the order of battle, and open the action at such time as they thought proper. Their officers lost control of them, and would plaintively say that if they could but enforce obedience in their men they would march through France from end to end.

This insubordination was their ruin. The French, who were their chief employers, at last lost all patience with them, and gave them at Marignano, (1515), a lesson which they did not speedily forget. The suppression of this mutiny, which was in fact a two days' battle of the most desperate description, cost the Swiss twelve thousand men; and it speaks volumes for the fine qualities that were in them that the defeat attached them more closely than ever to the cause of France. But the spell of their invincibility was broken, and two more severe defeats at the hands of a rival infantry at Bicocca, (1522), and Pavia, (1525), destroyed their prestige for ever. Nevertheless they were superb soldiers, and as their good fortune delivered them from a meeting with the English archers, who would certainly have riddled their huge bristling battalion through and through, they became as they deserved the fathers of modern infantry. Let it be noted that they marched in step to the music of fife and drum, that they carried a colour in each company, and that several of the cantons carried a huge horn, whose sound was the signal for all to rally around it.

It was not to be expected that the Swiss should long enjoy their monopoly as the infantry of Europe without exciting competition. In the last quarter of the fifteenth century arose the rivals who were to wrest their supremacy from them, namely, the *landsknechts* of Swabia, or as the contemporary English called them, the lance-knights of Almain, who were the direct forerunners of the modern German infantry. The records that survive of them are very full, and as it was through them that the teaching of the Swiss was carried into England, with results that are visible to this day, a brief study of their history is essential to the right understanding of the history of our own army.

The Swabian infantry was called into existence by the imperative necessity for preventing any potentate who might be so fortunate as to enlist the Swiss, from dictating his will to Europe. Swabia being the province next adjoining Switzerland was not unnaturally the first to learn the methods of her neighbour; and though at first all fighting men who imitated the tactics and equipment of the mountaineers were known by the generic name of Swiss, yet the Swabians, as if from the first to point the distinction between them and their rivals, took the name of *landsknechts*, men of the plain, as opposed to men of the mountains.

Maximilian the First, seeing how valuable such a force would be in the eternal contest of the House of Hapsburg against the House of Valois, more particularly since the Swiss were the firm allies of the French, gave them all possible countenance and encouragement; and very soon the *landsknechts* grew into one of the weightiest factors on the battlefields of Europe. Though mercenaries like the Swiss and the still earlier bands of Brabançons, and as such engaged on all sides and in all countries, they yet cherished not a little national sentiment; and the greatest of all their work was done in the service of the Empire.

When therefore the emperor needed infantry he issued a commission to some leader of repute to enlist for him a corps of *landsknechts*. The colonel, (*feld obrist*, now *oberst*), thus chosen thereupon selected a deputy or lieutenant colonel and captains, (*hauptmann*, the Germans wisely cling to these old titles, and preserve them), according to the number of men required, and bade them help him to raise his regiment. Then the fifes and drums were sent into the district, with a copy of the emperor's commission, to gather recruits. The recruits came, gave in their names and birthplaces to the muster-master, were informed of the time and place of assembly, and received a piece of money, (*laufgeld*), conduct-money as the English called it, to pay the expense of his journey thither and to bind the bargain. Here we draw a step closer to the Queen's shilling.

At the assembly the men were formed in two ranks, facing inwards. An arch, (reminiscence of the Roman *jugum*), was built by planting two halberds into the ground and laying a pike across them, and then every man passed singly beneath it under the eye of the muster-master and of his assistants, who watched every one sharply, rejecting all who were physically deficient or imperfectly armed, and above all taking care that no man should pass through twice, nor the same arms be shown by two different men. For captains were still unscrupulous, and were ever striving to show more men on their roll than they could produce in the flesh, and put the pay that they drew for them into their own pockets. So old was the trick and so deep-rooted the habit, that even in Hawkwood's bands the legitimate method of increasing a captain's pay was to allow him a certain number of fictitious men, called *mortes payes* (dead heads), and permit him to draw wages for them. This practice in a legitimised form continued in our own army within the memory of living men.

Four hundred men was the usual number assigned to a company, (*fähnlein*, flag or ensign), of *landsknechts*, but there was as yet no certainty either in the strength of companies themselves or in the number of them that were comprised within a regiment. The muster, (corruption of the French *monstre*, Latin *monstrare*, so to pass muster is to pass inspection), over, the men formed a ring round the colonel, who read aloud to them the conditions of service and the rate of pay, including under the former all the ordinary points of discipline. The men thereupon raised their hands, and with three fingers uplifted, swore by the Trinity that they would obey.

The colonel then called into the ring the officers whom he had selected to be ensigns, (*fähnlein*), and delivered to each the colour of his company, exhorting him to defend it to the death. Nor must it be supposed that the ensign was then the beardless boy with which our own later experience has accustomed us to identify the title. He was rather a hardened, grizzled old warrior, who could be trusted at all critical times to rally the men around him. Pursuant to Oriental tradition, the fife and drum of each company were under the ensign's immediate orders, so that the position of the colour might always be known by sound if not by sight. The flag itself, which gave the officer his title, bore some colour or device chosen by the colonel, and among the landsknechts was always very large and voluminous, probably to contrast with the flags of the Swiss, which were the smallest in Europe. The *landsknechts* prided themselves on the grace and skill with which they handled these huge banners, and indeed all the dandyism (if the term may be allowed) observable in later years in the manipulation of the colour may be traced to them.

This ceremony over, the various companies separated and formed each a distinct ring round its captain and ensign. The captain then selected his lieutenant, (*stellvertreter*, since abandoned for "*leutnant*."), and calling him under the colours bade the men obey him. He then chose also his chaplain and quartermaster, and having added to these a surgeon his patronage was exhausted. The men were then handed over to the senior non-commissioned officer, (*feldwebel*, the colour-sergeant), a very important person, who was responsible for all drill and for the posting of all guards, and received his appointment directly from the colonel. Under his guidance the company elected a sergeant, who then in turn selected himself an assistant, (*gemeinwebel*); the assistant then chose a reconnoitrer, (*fourier*), and the reconnoitrer a quartermaster-sergeant.

Finally, the company was distributed into files, (*rot*), 5 of ten men apiece, which selected each of them a file-leader, (*rottmeister*), who, though he received no extra pay, enjoyed certain privileges within his file, such as the right to a bed to himself in quarters and the like. (Sir Walter Scott in the *Legend of Montrose* has inexplicably confounded the word with *Rittmeister*, which is a very different thing; a rare mistake with him). With his election, the file being the unit of the company, the hierarchy was complete.

It is unnecessary to trouble the reader with a list of the regimental staff, but a word must be said of the provost. His principal function was the maintenance of discipline, for which purpose he was provided with a staff of gaolers and an executioner, and his title is still attached to the same duties in the English army of today. But apart from this, it was his office to fix the tariff of prices of goods sold by the sutlers who accompanied the regiment. It was a most difficult and dangerous duty, for if he fixed the price too high the men became discontented and mutinous, and if too low the sutlers deserted the camp and left it to provide for itself, which was an alternative little less formidable than the other.

In consideration of the perils of his office the provost received certain perquisites in addition to his salary, such as the tongue of every beast slaughtered and an allowance for every cask broached, and even so was none too well paid. (It is a curious sign of the combination of his functions, that in every standing camp the provost erected a gallows, which served to mark both the extent of his authority and the site of the marketplace, or as we should call it, canteen). It is hardly necessary to point out that in this commercial side of the provost's duties there lies the germ of our modern canteen, wherein the practice of taking perquisites, though strictly forbidden, still prevails among canteen-stewards.

The duties of another officer, whose name must be written down in the original, the *hurenweibel*, show the early methods of coping with a difficulty which particularly besets our Indian army. Every regiment of landsknechts was accompanied by a number of followers on the march; and although by strict rule no woman was allowed to accompany a man except his lawful wife, yet we hear without surprise that there were many women following the colours whose status was not recognised by the rule above referred to. The poor creatures led a hard life. The washing, cooking, scavenging, and all manner of unpleasant duties, as well as the more congenial task of nursing the sick and wounded, was entrusted to them, and in case of a siege they were required to make the fascines and gabions. Their masters treated them very brutally, and as every colonel naturally wished to cut down their numbers as low as possible, no pains were spared to make their lives a burden to them. Over all this rabble the *hurenweibel* was king, the sceptre of his office being a thick stick called a "straightener," (*vergleicher*), which he used unmercifully.

Yet these followers loved the life and tramped after their lords all over Europe, increasing their numbers as they went; the boys as they grew up being employed to carry the men's weapons or harness on the march. Such boys, or rather fags, were called in French *goujats*, and are a curious feature in the armies of the time. The greatest of all *goujats*, if legend may be trusted, was Thomas Cromwell, the Hammer of the Monks.

For the trial of military offences a board of justices accompanied each distinct body, but there were some corps of *landsknechts* that enjoyed the privilege of the trial of the long pikes, (*Recht der langen Spiesse*), which gave the rank and file sole jurisdiction in respect of crimes that brought disgrace on the regiment. In such cases the provost laid his complaint; and the ensigns, thrusting their flags point downward into the ground, vowed that they would never fly them again until the blot on the fair name of the regiment was removed. The culprit was then tried according to a certain fixed procedure by his comrades alone, without the intervention of any officer.

If he were found guilty, the men drew themselves up in two ranks, north and south, facing inwards; the ensigns, with colours flying, posted themselves at the east end of the lane thus formed, and the prisoner was brought to the west. The ensigns then exhorted him to play the man and make bravely for the colours, and the provost, clapping him thrice on the shoulder in the name of the Trinity, bade him run. Then the doomed man plunged into the lane, and every comrade plied pike and halberd and sword on him as he passed. The swifter he ran the sooner came the end, and as he lay hewn, mangled, and bleeding, gasping out his life, his comrades kneeled down together and prayed God to rest his soul. Then all rose and filed in silence three times round the corpse, and at the last the musketeers fired over it three volleys in the name of the Trinity.

The strength of a regiment of *landsknechts* varied very greatly. There might be thirty companies or there might be ten; the total force sometimes reached ten or twelve thousand men, and in such a case was frequently strengthened by a contingent of artillery. The weapons were the pike, the halberd, and a proportion of firearms, which last tended constantly to increase. Every man found his own arms, and the

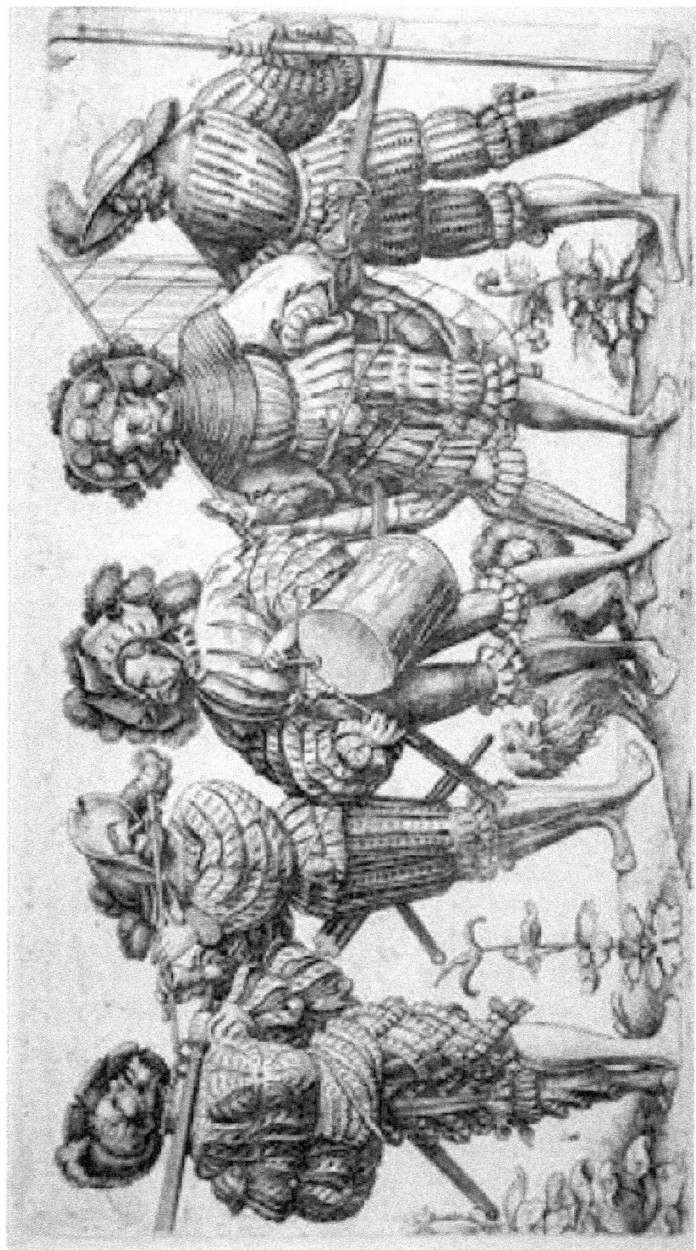

dress of the *landsknechts*, being that which it pleased each man best to wear, was generally both fantastic and extravagant, for they had all the soldier's ambition to let their light shine before women.

Maximilian's courtiers were so jealous of their gorgeous apparel that they begged him to forbid it, but the emperor was far too sensible to do anything so foolish. "Bah!" he said, "this is the cheese with which we bait our trap to catch such mice," a sentiment which English officers will still endorse. Not all the prejudices of dying feudalism could induce Maximilian to discourage his new infantry; on the contrary, meeting a regiment once on the march he dismounted, shouldered a pike, and marched with them for the rest of the day. It is worth noting that the drum-beat of the landsknechts, whereof they were extremely proud, probably the selfsame beat as that to which Maximilian strode along that day, still preludes the marches of our own military bands. (A roll on the two first beats of the bar, a single note on the third, and silence on the fourth).

The drill of the *landsknechts* was probably crude enough. There was no exercise for pike or halberd, and there is no sign of the complicated manoeuvres that were so common at the opening of the seventeenth century; but as they always fought, like the Swiss, in huge masses, there was probably little occasion for these. The men fell in by files, probably at sufficient distance and interval to allow every man to turn right or left about on his own ground; but for action they were closed up tight in vast battalions far too unwieldly for any evolution. Moreover, few of the officers knew anything of drill. They were selected for bravery and experience, no doubt, in some cases, but not for military knowledge; and it is the more probable that the colonels, according to custom, sold the position of officer to the highest bidder, since Maximilian could rarely furnish them with money for their preliminary expenses. The one duty expected without fail of officers was that they should be foremost in the fight, and as a rule they one and all took their place in the front rank with the colonel for centre, and, armed like their men, showed the way into the enemy's battalion.

Not one remained on a horse in action, though he might ride regularly on the march; and indeed the *landsknechts* disliked to see an officer mounted on anything larger than a pony at any time, admitting no reason for an infantryman to ride a good horse except that he might run away the faster. The duties of officers being thus defined, it is easy to see why the colonel reserved to himself the appointment of the colour-sergeants, for they were practically the only men who knew anything of drill or manoeuvre. The colonel might prescribe the formation of his battalion for action, but only the colour-sergeants could execute it; and hence arose the rule that sergeants should be armed with no weapon but a halberd, since any heavier weapon would impede them in the eternal running up and down the ranks which was imposed on them by their peculiar duty. The influence of these traditions was still visible in our army until quite recently. But a few years have passed since sergeants shouldered their rifles as though they carried a different weapon from the men, and officers have only lately ceased to depend on them greatly in matters of drill.

Such was the new infantry of Europe at the close of the fifteenth and the opening of the sixteenth centuries, not yet perfected, but advancing rapidly to an efficiency and importance such as had for many centuries been unknown in Europe. And now the nations poured down into the fair land of Italy to teach each other in that second birthplace of all arts the new-born art of war. France was the first that came; and few armies have caused greater wonder in Europe than that which marched with Charles the Eighth through Florence in 1496. The work begun for the expulsion of the English from France had been steadily continued. Louis the Eleventh had hired Swiss sergeants to drill his infantry, and Picardie, the senior regiment of the old French line, was already in potential existence.

But it was not these, but other men who set the Florentines at gaze. For there were to be seen the Scottish archers, the finest body-guard alike for valour and for stature in the world, the Swiss, marching by with stately step and incredible good order, the chivalrous gentlemen of France, mailed from top to toe and gorgeous in silken tabards, riding in all the pride of Agincourt avenged, mounted archers less heavy but more workmanlike as befitted light cavalry, and lastly a great train of brass artillery, cannons and culverins, and falcons, the largest weighing six thousand pounds and mounted on four wheels, the smallest made for shot no bigger than a doctor's pills and travelling on two wheels only. Already the quick-witted French had thought out the principle of the limber, and had made two wheels of their heavy guns removable. Already too they had trained the drivers of the lighter ordnance to move as swiftly as light cavalry. (See the account in *Paul Jove*).

We cannot follow this army through the triumphs and the disasters of the next half century, but we must needs glance briefly at the rapid progress of French military organisation. Louis the Twelfth took the improvement of his foot-soldiers seriously in hand and increased the number of the companies, or bands as they were called, that had been begun by the bands of Picardy. The number of these bands, permanent and temporary, demanded the appointment of an officer who should be intermediary between the general and the captains of independent companies. About the year 1524 such an officer was established with the new title of colonel, and the companies placed under his command were said, in French, to be under his regiment.

★★★★★★

We need not enter into the controversy whether the word was derived from *columna* or *corona* or from neither. For a century or more it was written indifferently colonel or coronel, to which last the modern English pronunciation is doubtless to be traced. Brantome writes always *couronnel*; Milton in his famous sonnet gives the word the dignity of the three syllables. Some say that it was borrowed from the landsknechts, but this is a palpable error. (See a paper by Mr. Julian Corbett, *American Hist. Review*, Oct. 1896, "The Colonel and his Command").

★★★★★★

The word soon grew to be used in a collective sense, and such and such companies under Colonel A.'s regiment became known simply as Colonel A.'s regiment. The colonel had a company of his own, but having no leisure to attend to it made it over to a captain, who was called the colonel's lieutenant or lieutenant-colonel. Another company was commanded by the sergeant-major, the word sergeant, which we met with first at the very beginning, having come into use in France with a new meaning in the year 1485.

As already mentioned in speaking of the *landsknechts*, the name of sergeant became for some reason bound up with the functions of drill, and the sergeant-major was to the regiment what the sergeant was to the company. He was therefore the only officer who remained on his horse in action, his duties compelling him continually to gallop from company to company for the correction of bad formation, and for the ordering of ranks and files. It will be seen that the sergeant-major, or as we now call him major, originally did the work which is now performed in England by the adjutant.

Captain was of course an old title, and had been used for the chief of a band in France ever since 1355, having been borrowed possibly from the free companies. The captain's *locum tenens* or lieutenant had been instituted by the reforms of Charles the Seventh in 1444, and together with him his standard-bearer or ensign, (French *enseigne*; Lat.

101

insigne, signum), but there were other junior officers who came later even than the colonels to supplement the new military vocabulary. In 1534 we encounter for the first time *fouriers*, caps *d'escouade*, and *lancepessades*. The first of these, which existed for a time in the corrupted form *furrier*, has passed from the English language. (But not until after the Seven Years' War, when Lord George Sackville applied for a "furrier.") The second is the French form of the Italian *capo de squadra*, head of the square, a reminiscence of the days when men were formed into square blocks, squads or squadrons, which passed into *caporal* and so into our English corporal.

The third, again a French form of the Italian *lanz pesato*, signified originally a man-at-arms whose horse had been killed and who was therefore compelled to march with the foot. Being a superior person, he was not included among the common infantry-men but held this distinctive and superior rank, whence in due time was derived the prefix of lance to the titles of sergeant and corporal. Finally, in the year 1550 foot-soldiers in France began to be called by the collective name of *fanterie* or *infanterie*. This word, too, was a corruption from the Italian, for Italian commanders used to speak of their troops as their boys, *fanti*, and collectively as *fanteria*; and from them the term passed into all the languages of Europe. Nothing could better commemorate the situation of Italy in the sixteenth century as at once the cockpit of the nations and the school of the new art of war.

But before leaving France there is another aspect of her military institutions to be touched on. After the death of Francis the First, and particularly during the period of the religious wars, the discipline and tone of the French army underwent woeful deterioration. Captains from the first had been proprietors of their companies, which indeed were sometimes sold at auction by the colonel to the highest bidder; and, as they received a bounty in proportion to the numbers that they could show on their rolls, the rascality and corruption were appalling. The enforcement of strict discipline was bound to cause desertion, and every deserter meant a man the less on the captain's roll and a sum the less in the captain's pocket. No effort therefore was made to restrain the misbehaviour of soldiers when off duty; they were allowed to rob and plunder at their own sweet will, and they had the more excuse since they were encouraged thus to indemnify themselves for the pay stolen from them by their officers.

This recognised system of pillage was known as *picorée*, a word which has passed through the English language in the form of pickeer.

(We even find the word incarnated by French writers as the strumpet Madame Picorée). Yet another method there was among many of falsifying the muster-rolls, namely on the day of inspection to collect any yokels or men that could be found, thrust a pike into their hands, and present them as soldiers. They were duly passed by the muster-master, and as soon as his back was turned were dismissed, having served their purpose of securing their pay for the illicit gain of the captain till next muster.

Such men were called *passe-volans*, a word which also was received into the military terminology of Europe, and like *mortes-payes* received at last official recognition. It must not be thought that such abuses were confined to France, but it is significant that she was the country to find names for them (As a matter of fact-these abuses do seem to have been more flagrant in France than elsewhere, owing no doubt to the demoralisation caused by the religious wars. See Brantôme, and the *Memoirs* of Sully). Nor must the reader be unduly impatient over the mention of these details in the military history of foreign nations. The English soldier for the next century and more is going to school, where like all pupils he will learn both good and evil; and it is impossible to follow his progress unless we know something of his schoolfellows as well as of his tutors.

Last of the nations let us glance at Spain, at the close of the fifteenth century just emerging triumphant from eight centuries of warfare against the Moors and girding herself for a great and magnificent career. Her training in war had been against an Oriental foe, swift, active, and cunning, and it is not surprising that when first she entered the field of Italy and met the. massive columns of the Swiss at Seminara, (1495), she should have given way before them. But at the head of the Spanish troops was a man of genius, Gonsalvo of Cordova, who was quick to learn from his enemies. Confining himself for a time to the guerilla warfare which he understood the best, he mingled pikes among the short swords and bucklers which were the distinctive weapons of the Spanish infantry, and within a year had gained his first victory over the Swiss.

His next campaign, Atella 1496, found him with a body of *landsknechts* in his pay, when he quickly perceived the possibilities that lay not only in the pikes but still more in the fire-arms which they brought with them. Before the year, (1503), was past he had routed Swiss infantry and French cavalry in two brilliant actions at Cerignola and on the Garigliano, and fairly driven them out of Naples. He then set himself to remodel the Spanish foot by the experience which he had gathered in his later campaigns, and this with full appreciation of the moral and physical peculiarities of his countrymen. Thus though it was in the Spanish tongue that the pike was first named the queen of weapons, yet the value of the sword in the hand of a supple active people was never overlooked, and at Ravenna, (1512), no less than Cerignola the rush of nimble stabbing Spaniards under the hedge of pikes had proved fatal to the lumbering unwieldy Teuton.

Still more remarkable was the rapid development of the power of musketry in Spanish hands. At Bicocca, (1522), the Marquis Pescayra met the attack of a gigantic Swiss battalion by drawing up a number of small squares or squadrons of Spanish arquebusiers in front of his own battalion of pikes. His instructions were that not a shot should be fired without orders, a fact that points to early excellence in what is now called fire-discipline, but that each front rank should fire a volley by word of command and having done so should file away to the rear to reload, leaving the remaining ranks to do the like in succession. The results of this manoeuvre were disastrous to the Swiss; and this ingenious method of maintaining a continuous fire of musketry was the law in Europe for the next century and a half. In fact, if it were necessary to fix an arbitrary date for the first really effective use of small firearms in the battlefield the day of Bicocca might well be selected.

But we must not fail to note concurrently the drill and discipline which made Pescayra's evolution possible. Three years later, 1525, at the famous Battle of Pavia, this same skilful soldier attempted a still bolder innovation with his arquebusiers, and with astonishing success. Being threatened with a charge of French heavy cavalry (men-at-arms) he deployed fifteen hundred of his marksmen in skirmishing order before his front, who, taking advantage of every shelter and moving always with great nimbleness and activity, maintained a galling fire as the cavalry advanced, and finally, taking refuge under the pikes of the battalions which were drawn up in their support, smashed the unfortunate French as effectively as the English archers at Creçy.

In truth, the effect of this daring experiment on military minds in Europe was hardly less than that of Creçy itself. Henry, Duke of Guise, (see conversation Brantôme vol. 1), an excellent soldier, was so much struck by its success that he showed how the principle might be indefinitely extended and find ultimate shape, as many years later it did, in the formation of distinct corps of light-infantry. His own attempt to organise such a body in France was however a failure, and the Spanish arquebusiers long held their own as the first in Europe, a proud position which they had most worthily gained.

The remarkable prowess of the Spanish infantry soon made it popular with the nation. The cavalry, in the palmy days of chivalry the most gorgeous in Europe, lost its attraction for the young nobles, who enrolled themselves as private soldiers in the ranks of the foot, and carried pike and arquebus with the meanest of the people. Charles the Fifth himself once shouldered a piece, and marched, like Maximilian, in the ranks, until ordered by the commander-in-chief, (Marquis del Vasto, of the same family as Pescayra), of his own appointment not to expose himself to unnecessary danger, when like a good soldier he at once obeyed orders.

And this leads us to another eminent feature of the Spaniards, the excellence of their discipline. English and French contemporary writers, (Roger Williams and Tavannes), agreed that they owed their victories to nothing else but obedience and good order, for that they were not in themselves remarkable as a fighting people. Roger Williams says:—

> I am persuaded that ten thousand of our nation would beat thirty thousand of theirs out of the field, excepting some three thousand, the choicest of the army, that are in the Low Countries.

Gonsalvo was the man who had laid the foundation of this discipline, and it was worthily maintained by his successors. Charles the Fifth went so far in his respect for it as always to salute the gallows whenever he happened to pass them. And yet there are no signs of extraordinary brutality in the Spanish army, but on the contrary most remarkable tokens of good fellowship between officers and men, and of healthy *esprit de corps*. There was a system of comradeship which was the envy of all Europe. The two officers of each company, the captain and ensign, (in Spanish *alferez*), would each take to themselves and entertain from three to six comrades from the young nobles who served in the ranks; sergeants would also take one or two such comrades, and the privates formed little messes among themselves in like manner, with the result, unique in those days, that fighting and brawling were unknown in a Spanish camp. Quite as striking was the pride which the old soldiers took in themselves and their profession.

It is recorded, (*Brantôme*), that a party of Spanish recruits, who had arrived at Naples, ragged, slovenly, and unkempt, and were staring about them in a clownish and unsoldierly fashion, were at once taken in hand by the old soldiers, who lent them good clothes, made them tidy, and taught them proper manners.

For the rest the Spaniards originated a system which, though it now seems obvious enough, was in those days a new thing. It consisted simply in the maintenance of a nucleus, or as we should now call it a depot, of trained men sufficiently numerous to teach recruits their duty. All recruits were trained in the garrisons at home, and from thence passed into the ranks of the regiment wherein they were needed; and every draft so disposed of was immediately replaced by an equal number of new recruits. When it is remembered that, according to the ideas of the time, seven thousand trained infantry and three thousand cavalry were judged sufficient to leaven an army of fifty thousand men, the strength which her system of recruiting gave to Spain is not easily exaggerated.

The trained regiments of Spanish infantry were but four, and their united strength did not exceed seven thousand men, but their ranks were always full. The number of companies into which they were distributed was uncertain, and the strength of the companies themselves varied from one hundred and fifty to three hundred men, a curious defect in the most perfect organisation of the time. Lastly, the Spanish regiments were known by the name of *tercios*, a term with which the reader must not quarrel, as he will encounter it on the battlefield of Naseby. (*Tercio*, like colonel, is a riddle which defies solution. It means a third, but a third of what is unknown—see Mr. Julian Corbett's paper, quoted earlier).

Not less remarkable than their forwardness in organisation and discipline was the ready quickness of the Spaniard in the improvement of fire-arms. The primitive hand-gun, as I have already said, differed little except in size from the smaller cannon of the time. It consisted simply of a barrel with a vent at the top, and though indeed attached to a wooden stock had no lock of any description. Hand-guns were often made so short that they could be held even by a mounted man with one hand and fired with the other. Match-cord or tinder for purposes of firing the charge by the vent was already in full use, (1475).

The next step was to increase the length of the barrel and support it on a forked rest, a plan introduced by the Spaniards at Charles the Fifth's invasion of the Milanese in 1521. Ten years later a vast stride was made by the substitution of a pan at the side of the barrel for a vent at the top, and by the addition of a grip to the stock to hold the match-cord, which was brought in contact with the pan by pressing a trigger. In a word, the barrel was fitted with a lock.

An extremely ingenious Italian in the French service, Filippo Strozzi, then took the improvement of fire-arms in hand, copying however, as always, from the Spanish model. The bore of the harquebus (for the primitive German *hakenbuchse* had by this time found its permanent corrupted form) was by him enlarged to bear a heavier charge and carry a larger bullet; and so perfect was the workmanship of the Milanese gunsmiths whom he employed that he succeeded in killing a man at four hundred and a horse at five hundred paces. The stock being long and the recoil very severe, men suffered not a little from bruises and contusions with this weapon; but its efficiency was proved. Strozzi also introduced another Spanish improvement, namely the practice of making all his arquebuses of one bore, which, though it now sounds obvious enough, waited for some years to find general acceptance in Europe. Hence the weapons were known as arquebuses of calibre, which phrase in England was soon shortened simply to calivers. These however were arms of small bore: it was, as usual, the Spaniards who were the first to arm their infantry with muskets of large calibre.

******

In a MS. treatise in the Record Office, of date 1570, the bore recommended is 28 bullets to the pound. This remained the standard bore in the French army all through the wars of Louis XIV.

Musket is simply the word mosquito. Larger weapons were called drakes, falcons, and the like, and the smaller therefore after the lesser flying creatures.

******

Alva was the man who introduced them, (1567), and the rebels of the Low Countries the first who felt their power.. It needed but the substitution of a flint-lock for a match, and the abolition of the rest, to turn this weapon into Brown Bess, never so famous in English hands as in the battlefields of Alva's home. Bandoliers and cartridges had long been known to the Spaniards, and even to the French, (*Mem.* de Vieilleville), before the middle of the sixteenth century, so that the general progress in arms and equipment was rapid.

But the weapons had hardly been improved for infantry before cavalry also began to crave for them. The simplest method of course was to place pike and arquebus in the hands of mounted men and turn them into mounted infantry, which was duly done in the French army by Piero Strozzi in 1543, and has earned him the title of the father of dragoons, (this again is a word which defies the skill of the etymologist). But still earlier in the century there had grown up in Germany a new kind of cavalry, called by the simple name of *Reiters*, which had perfected the smaller fire-arms, the *petronel*, (*poitrinal*, so called because it was held against the chest), and the pistol, and had finally adopted the latter for its principal weapon. The result was an important revolution in the whole tactics of cavalry.

Mention has already been made of the abandonment, at the close of the fifteenth century, of the dense column of mounted men-at-arms in favour of the less cumbrous formation in line, or as it was called *en haye*. The lance being still the principal arm of the cavalry, the freedom of movement gained by the change brought the attack of horse much nearer to the shock-action which is the rule at the present day. The new formation had, however, its disadvantages, for in the imperfect state of military discipline there was no certainty that the whole line would charge home. Retirement was so easy that cowards would drop back, feigning to bleed at the nose, to have lost a stirrup or cast a shoe, (*Mem.* de La Noue), while men of spirit, and this was especially true of the impetuous French, would race to be the first into the enemy's squadron, and from premature increase of speed would arrive at the shock in loose order, and with horses blown and exhausted. So well was this defect realised that a shrewd French officer, Gaspard de Tavannes, at the Battle of Renty, 1554, deliberately reverted to the old dense column and overthrew every line that he met.

Yet another cause was contributing to restore the column as the favourite formation for the attack of cavalry. With the steady improvement in fire-arms, the bullet became more and more potent in velocity and penetration, and increasingly difficult to fend off by means of armour. It must never be forgotten that a bullet-wound, for a century and more after the introduction of fire-arms, generally meant death. The primitive surgery of the time, misled by the livid appearance of the edges of the wound, pronounced bullets to be in their nature venomous, and treated the hurt somewhat" as a snake's bite, with such tortures of boiling oil and other descriptions of cautery as are sickening even to read of.

Wise men took refuge in the virtues of cold water, and kept the surgeons at a safe distance. "Trust a doctor and he will kill you; mistrust him and he will insult you," wrote a Frenchman, (Tavannes, vol. i.),

Reiters

who had suffered much from the profession. But above all, men relied on prevention rather than cure; so to keep bullets out of their bodies they made their armour heavier and heavier, covering themselves with stithies, to use the words of contemptuous critics, (Tavannes, La Nou), till they could neither endure swift movements themselves nor find horses that could maintain any pace under the burden. (It is curious to compare the parallel contest of armoured ships and artillery at the present time). It was obvious therefore that if cavalry was to act by shock, the shock must be, as in former days, that of ponderous weight rather than of high speed.

Moreover, quite apart from all questions of formation there was much in the prevailing tactics of infantry to encourage cavalry to change the lance for the pistol. Huge square battalions, bristling with eighteen-foot pikes and garnished with musketeers, were not easily to be broken by a charge, but presented a large mark at a fairly safe range to the mounted pistolier. Thus all circumstances conspired to favour a great and radical reform in the tactics of cavalry, the change not only from line to column, but from shock to missile action. When once the pistol was recognised as the principal weapon of the horsemen, it was obvious that all other tactical considerations must give way to the maintenance of a continuous fire.

To this end there was but one system known, namely the old method of Pescayra, that the front rank should fire first and file away to the rear to reload, leaving successive ranks to come up in its place, and go through the same performance in turn. Plainly, therefore, a reversion to the old dense column, as great in depth as in breadth of front, was imperative. It was accordingly reintroduced, and from its quadrate outline was called by the name of a squadron, which from this period tends to become a term applied exclusively to cavalry. Massed together in such squadrons men could move slowly and steadily, willingly sacrificing speed that they might take the better and surer aim.

Such was the new principle brought forward early in the sixteenth century by the mounted mercenary bands of Germany, and with ever-increasing success. Very soon the *reiters* become recognised as a valuable force, and received from Charles the Fifth something of the encouragement that the *landsknechts* had gained from Maximilian. The military aspirants of the Empire, forsaking the ranks of the once honoured infantry, hastened to enrol themselves among the new horse, and the *landsknechts* decayed that the *reiters* might flourish. That the new service was as honourable as the old may be doubted, for the *reiters* were proverbial for brutality, and their practice of blackening their faces betokens something of a ruffianly spirit; but, be that as it might, they forced their system, in spite of bitter opposition, upon the cavalry of Europe, and from the day of the Battle of St. Quentin, (1557), may be said to have assured their evil supremacy.

It is therefore necessary to glance briefly at their organisation. The tactical unit was the squadron, which was of uncertain strength, varying from one hundred to three or even five hundred men. The officers were a captain, (*rittmeister*), lieutenant, ensign, (*fähnrich*), and quartermaster, (*fourrier*), and the staff was completed by a chaplain, a sergeant, (*wachtmeister*), and a trumpeter. As every man brought his own equipment there was no precise uniformity, but it may be assumed as certain that all wore complete defensive armour to the waist, and some even to mid-thigh.

For offensive purposes a pistol, or rather a brace of pistols, was indispensable. As in the case of the *landsknechts*, all matters of drill were the business of the sergeant, but it does not appear that the *reiters* ever attained great proficiency in manoeuvre. Thus in action the successive ranks of the squadron seem to have been unable to file to the rear except to their left, so that it was impossible to post them on the right wing without bringing them into collision with the centre of their own line of battle. The trumpeters, it is worth noting, were required to be masters of but six calls,—Saddle, Mount, Mess, March, Alarm, Charge,—of which the French employed the first two and last two only. We shall presently make further acquaintance with these six calls, but it is sufficient meanwhile to call attention to their existence in the middle of the sixteenth century. The *reiters* however, should not be forgotten, for though not comparable to the *landsknechts* for quality as troops, they furnished the model for the first famous regiment of English cavalry. (. The particulars of the *reiters'* organisation are taken from the Kriegsbuch of Leonard Fronsberger, 1566).

Lastly, let me close this necessarily brief and imperfect account of the renascence of the art of war by a remark which should perhaps have come first rather than last. Amid all the innovations which went forward during the sixteenth century in the province of armament, classical models reigned supreme in organisation and manoeuvre. The whole story of the renascence resembles, if I may be allowed to use the metaphor, a long musical passage in pedal point, on the deep bass note of classical tradition. For this the revival of classical learning was doubtless responsible. When generals celebrated a triumph, as more than one general did, in the Roman manner after a victory, the pageant could hardly be complete without the presence of legions; and when Machiavelli declared that the Swiss tactics were those of the Macedonian *phalanx*, military students could be in no doubt where to seek out models for their own imitation. Francis the First adopted in 1534 both the name and organisation of the Roman legions for a time, while no military writer omitted to recommend the Roman ideal to aspirants of his profession.

Every soldier steeped himself in ancient military lore, and quoted the Hipparchicus of Xenophon, (it is just possible that Xenophon's example may have favoured the abandonment of shock for missile tactics in cavalry), and the Tactics of Ælian, the Commentaries of Caesar and the expeditions of Alexander, Epaminondas' heavy infantry and Pompey's discipline. A Frenchman could not even praise the merits of the Englishman as a marine without calling him *epibates*. In a word Europe for two centuries, went forth to war with the newest pattern of musket in hand, and a brain stocked with maxims from Frontinus and Vegetius and Æneas Poliorceticus, and with examples from Plutarch and Livy and Arrian. She might well have found worse instructors; but their lessons were for the most part imperfectly understood, and their broad principles seldom correctly deduced or intelligently applied. An opportunity was thus afforded for the demon of pedantry, which was eagerly and joyfully seized. Nevertheless, the present armies of Europe still double their ranks and files, by whatever name they may designate the evolution, after the manner prescribed by Ælian, and by him borrowed, it is likely, from the stern martinets of ancient Lacedæmon.

CHAPTER 7

Accession of the Tudors

The accession of the Tudors to the throne of England marks an important period in our military history. The nation, after thirty years of furious internal war, during which it had lost all sense of national honour, began to settle down once more to a life of peace, and awoke to the fact that England was now no more than an insular power. France was lost to her except Calais, but Calais was something more than a mere sentimental possession. It was the bridge-head that secured to the English their passage of the Channel; and while it remained in the hands of an English garrison there was always the temptation to engage in Continental wars and to employ the army for purposes of aggression as well as of defence.

Still the prospects of regaining the ancestral possessions of the Plantagenets in France seemed so hopeless that the English sovereigns might well doubt whether it were not now time to give the navy the first and the army the second place; and this question, already half decided by the keen good sense of King Henry the Eighth, was finally determined by the loss of Calais itself. There was, of course, always a frontier to be guarded on the Tweed, but with the cessation of expeditions to France, which had invariably called the Scotch armies across the border, there was no longer the same danger of Scottish invasion; and moreover, England and Scotland were now beginning to draw closer together. Thus it would seem that after the death of Queen Mary there should have been little reason for the existence of an English army, and indeed it will be seen that the national force became in many respects lamentably deficient.

But meanwhile the wars of Europe changed from a contest between nation and nation to a death struggle between Catholic and Protestant. It was religion that drew the Scotch from their old alliance with the French to their former enemies the English; and it was religion which led the English to the battlefields of the Low Countries, where they learned the new art of war. The reign of the Tudor dynasty therefore falls for the purpose of this history into three periods, which are conveniently separated by the fall of Calais or the more familiar landmark of the accession of Elizabeth, and by the first departure of English volunteers to the Low Countries in 1572.

It is extremely difficult to discover the exact condition of England's military organisation when Henry the Seventh was fairly seated on the throne. The old feudal system, which had been turned by the nobles to such disastrous account for their own ends in the Civil War, seems to have been but half alive. Compositions, indents, and commissions of array had already weakened it in the past, and indents in themselves had been shown to be unsafe. The difficulties wherein Henry found himself are shown by two statutes imposing the obligation of military service on two new classes, namely holders of office, fees or annuities under the crown, or of honours and lands under the King's letters patent. It was stipulated that they should receive wages from the day of leaving their homes until the day of their return to them; but they were strictly forbidden to depart without leave, and their service was declared to be due both within the kingdom and without. But in fact the sovereign seems to have been driven back on the force which represented the old Saxon *fyrd*, and had its legal existence under the Statute of Winchester.

Noblemen and gentlemen could of course still show a body of retainers, but many, indeed most, of the ancient magnates had perished, and recent experience had shown the danger of permitting their retinue to become too powerful. A curious complication, to which I shall presently return, in the collapse of the old feudal service was the extreme dearth of good horses. Altogether everything tended to compel resort to the national militia as the principal military force of England. Two allowances to the levies of the shire seem to have been finally established in this reign, namely coat-money and conduct-money. The first, as its name denotes, helped the soldier to provide himself with clothing and was a step further towards uniform; and indeed it is possible that it was deliberately designed to exclude the liveries of the nobility, already condemned by statute, in favour of the national white with the red cross of St. George.

The conduct-money was simply the old allowance which was seen in the days of William Rufus, but which from henceforth apparently was refunded to the shire from the Exchequer. Both, however, though paid in advance to the soldier, were ultimately deducted from his pay, and are therefore of interest in the history of the British soldier's stoppages. Finally, we find indications of a stricter discipline in a statute that makes desertion while on service outside the kingdom into felony, and subjects captains who defraud men of their pay to forfeiture of goods and to imprisonment.

A few points remain to be mentioned before we pass to the reign of Henry the Eighth. The first was the establishment of that royal body-guard, 1485, which with its picturesque old dress and original title of Yeomen of the Guard still survives among us. (There were two kinds of soldiers, the gentleman soldier and the yeoman soldier. Hence the name points to the enlistment of men below the status of gentleman. The navy still has "Yeomen of the Signals.")

Though doubtless imitated from the Scottish Guard of the French kings, it is of greater interest as being composed not of aliens but of Englishmen, and as the first permanent corps of trained English soldiers in our history. Another smaller matter cannot be ignored without disrespect to military sentiment. After the victory of Bosworth Field Henry offered at the altar of St. Paul's Cathedral a banner charged with "a red fiery dragon" upon a field of white and green, the ensign of Cadwallader, the last of the British kings, from whom he was fond of tracing his descent. The scarlet of this red fiery dragon became from this time the royal livery, and was for the present reserved, together with purple, to the king's use alone.

★★★★★★

I must confess that this should be put forward rather as a conjecture than an assertion; but it is remarkable that Henry VIII. should have permitted the use of any colours to the Artillery Company except purple and scarlet. Green and white were the favourite Tudor colours, being used even in ribbons for the attachment of the Great Seal.

★★★★★★

But the green and white was more liberally distributed both to soldiers and mariners. A white jacket with the red cross of St. George had long been a common distinction of the English soldier, and the white as a colour of the Tudors now became so general that for a time "white coat "was used as a synonym for soldier.

Lastly must be noticed the definite establishment of the Office of Ordnance for the custody of military stores. The early history of the office is exceedingly obscure, and the existence of King Edward the Second's *artillator* hardly warrants us in assuming the permanent foundation of the department in the fourteenth century. The record of a Clerk of the Ordnance in 1418 sets the office on surer ground, and in 1483 the appointment of a Master-General advances it to a stage at which it becomes recognisable by us even at the present day; for the title of Master-General was held by John, Duke of Marlborough, and by Arthur, Duke of Wellington.

With Henry the Eighth we reach a new example in our history of an English soldier-king. Young, able, accomplished, and ambitious, he was strongly imbued with the military spirit, and possessed many qualities that must have made him a popular and might have made him a distinguished commander. He excelled in every exercise of arms; he was the finest archer in his kingdom; he had studied the art of war in the best authorities; he understood the conduct both of a siege and of a campaign; and lastly, he was no mean artillerist. This last attribute, however, he shared with several sovereigns of his time. Artillery was a favourite hobby with the crowned heads of Europe, possibly as a symbol of their military strength, for being unable to give themselves the pleasure of a great review owing to the inevitable confusion and expense, they were fain to console themselves with the several pieces, each one of them called by its pet name, that composed their park of ordnance.

Altogether Henry was a prince who bade fair to restore the military prestige of England. His first step was to increase his standing force by the creation of a second body-guard of men-at-arms, (*Cal. S. P.* 20th November 1509), composed of young men of noble blood; the reason given being that there were far too many such young men in the kingdom who were untrained in arms. The corps, as might have been expected with the best dressed sovereign in Europe, was so gorgeously arrayed that it perished after a few years under the weight of its own cost. His next act was more practical, a writ to the sheriffs for the better enforcement of the Statute of Winchester, which is interesting for its attempt to restore the command of the forces of the shore to their original holders, (*ibid.* 5th July 1511). Concurrently, however, we encounter a large number of the old-fashioned indents and commissions of array, all issued in prospect of English intervention in the eternal strife of the Hapsburgs and the Valois, (*ibid.* 3rd November 1509, 20th June, 1st July 1511, 8th April 1512. Rymer, vol. xiii.)

In 1512 an expedition was sent to the south of France, and there the defects of the army were lamentably seen. Although the importation of handguns and arquebuses shows that England was not blind to the progress of fire-arms in Europe, this force was armed principally if not exclusively with the old-fashioned bows and bills, and worse than all, these bows, which had been issued from the stores in the Tower, were found nearly all of them to be useless. Moreover, the victuals were "untruly served" to the men, their pay was withheld from them, and, acutest of all grievances, they could get no beer.

The Council of War, in which the command was vested, could never agree as to a plan of operations, and though it kept the men thus inactive made no attempt to drill or exercise" them. The natural result was a mutiny. One large band struck work for eightpence a day in lieu of the regular sixpence, several others swore that nothing should keep them from going home, and the disturbance was only quelled by the hanging of a ringleader, (*Cal. S. P.* 5th August 1512).

Henry seems to have had suspicions of the state of affairs, for in the same year Acts were passed to renew the existing statutes against desertion and fraud; though from the incessant re-enactment of these particular provisions it is clear that they were either easily evaded or negligently enforced. In the following year, however, Henry took the field in person in Normandy, (1513), where. his presence appears materially to have altered the complexion of affairs. His force was designed to have consisted of thirty thousand men, but was reduced by impending trouble with Scotland to less than half that number.

The details of its organisation are still extant, and it is curious to find that, after but two generations of severance from France, the French terms vanguard, battle, and rearguard have given place to foreward, mid-ward, and rear-ward. Another novelty is the addition of wings, which had formerly been attached to the vanguard only, to the midward also; which was clearly a new departure, (Stow). There is again a strong tendency, which after a year becomes a rule, to make the tactical units of uniform strength, one hundred men being the common establishment for a company. Every captain too has an officer under him called his petty captain, a name which appears in the statutes of the previous reign, and was not yet displaced by the title, as yet reserved to the king's deputies only, of lieutenant.

★★★★★★

Such at least is my impression. The commander-in-chief of a force not commanded by the king in person is styled the lieutenant or king's lieutenant. So also the commander of the body-guard is styled lieutenant, the king himself being captain. Compare the title, which we shall presently see introduced, of lord-lieutenant. But we meet also with the phrase lieutenant (*i.e.* commanding officer) of the rearguard or other of the three divisions in the army. The word is always used of a high office.

★★★★★★

The ensign does not yet make his appearance, for the grouping of companies is strictly territorial, and one standard apparently alone is allowed to each shire, (in 1542, however, Wallop constantly speaks of ensigns—State Papers, Henry VIII. vol. ix *anno* 1542). Every company, however, has the distinctive badge of its captain, and the archers of the King's Guard are dressed in uniform of white gaberdines. Lastly, there are in the army fifteen hundred Almains, the *landsknechts* of whom account was given in a previous section, eight hundred of whom, "all in a plump," marched immediately before the King. Possibly this place of honour was granted to them to kindle the emulation of the English, but more probably because Henry, following the evil example of the French, trusted more to trained mercenaries than to his own subjects. We shall constantly meet with such contingents of aliens among the English during the next forty years, until at last England awakes, like every other nation in Europe, to the truth that her own children, as carefully trained, are worth just double of the foreigners.

The most remarkable of the mounted men in this army were the Northern Horsemen, who, called into being at some uncertain period by the eternal forays on the Scottish border, now appear regularly on the strength of every expedition as perfectly indispensable. They were light cavalry, the first deserving the name ever seen in our army, and probably the very best in Europe. They wore defensive armour of back and breast and iron cap, carried lance and buckler or sometimes a bow, and were mounted on "nags" which were probably nearer thirteen than fourteen hands high. For duties of reconnaissance they were perfect, and they must be reckoned the first regular English horse that were the eyes and ears of the army. We shall see them at a later stage merged in a mounted body much resembling them, namely the demi-lances, which were destined, during the period of transition that is before us, to fill the place already almost vacated by the men-at-arms.

There is no need to dwell on the incidents of a not very eventful campaign. The panic flight of the French at the Battle of the Spurs upheld the old belief that they could not stand before the English; and the siege and capture of Terouenne under the personal direction of

Henry helped to confirm it. A fruitless attack on an English convoy, curiously resembling the Battle of the Herrings in its main features, also helped to maintain the ancient reputation of the English archers. Lastly, the siege of Tournay gave Henry an opportunity of showing off some of his new artillery. There were twelve huge pieces, called the twelve apostles, of which he was particularly proud; but as St. John stuck in the mud and was unfortunately captured, it is well not to say too much of them. But the French were by no means impressed with the appearance of their old enemies in the field. Fleuranges wrote in a patronising way:—

> The English are good men and fight well when parked in a strong position, but otherwise I make no great account of them.

But while Henry was plying his apostles against Tournay, some still older enemies of the nation had formed a very different opinion of the English. For in September 1513, Thomas, Earl of Surrey, met the Scots at Flodden Field, September 9, and dealt them a blow from which they never wholly recovered. The odds against the English were heavy, for they could bring but twenty-six thousand men against forty thousand or, as some say, eighty thousand Scots, and the position taken up by James the Fourth was so strong that Surrey could not venture to attack it. With ready intelligence he made a detour from south to north of the Scottish host, and James, who had not attempted to molest him during the movement, hurried down, fearful of being cut off from his base, to meet him in the open field. The sequel is an example of the helplessness of pedantry, even of the newest pattern, in the face of genuine military instinct. The Scotch had studied the methods of the *landsknechts*; they were armed principally with pikes; they were drawn up in five huge battalions, after the Swiss model, and they advanced to the attack in silence "after the Almain manner."

Lastly, they had with them some of the finest artillery hitherto seen, (*Cal. S.P.* 1513. 4460). Yet all this availed them nothing. The English too were formed, after a method which had lately come into fashion, in two divisions, foreward and rearward, each with two wings; but Surrey boldly wheeled both into one grand line, (*ibid.* 4441), holding but one small body of horse in reserve, and appears to have overlapped the cumbrous masses of the enemy. There is no need to give details of the battle; it began between four and five in the evening and was over in an hour. The English leaders seem to have shown not only bravery but skill. The English archers as usual wrought havoc against unar-

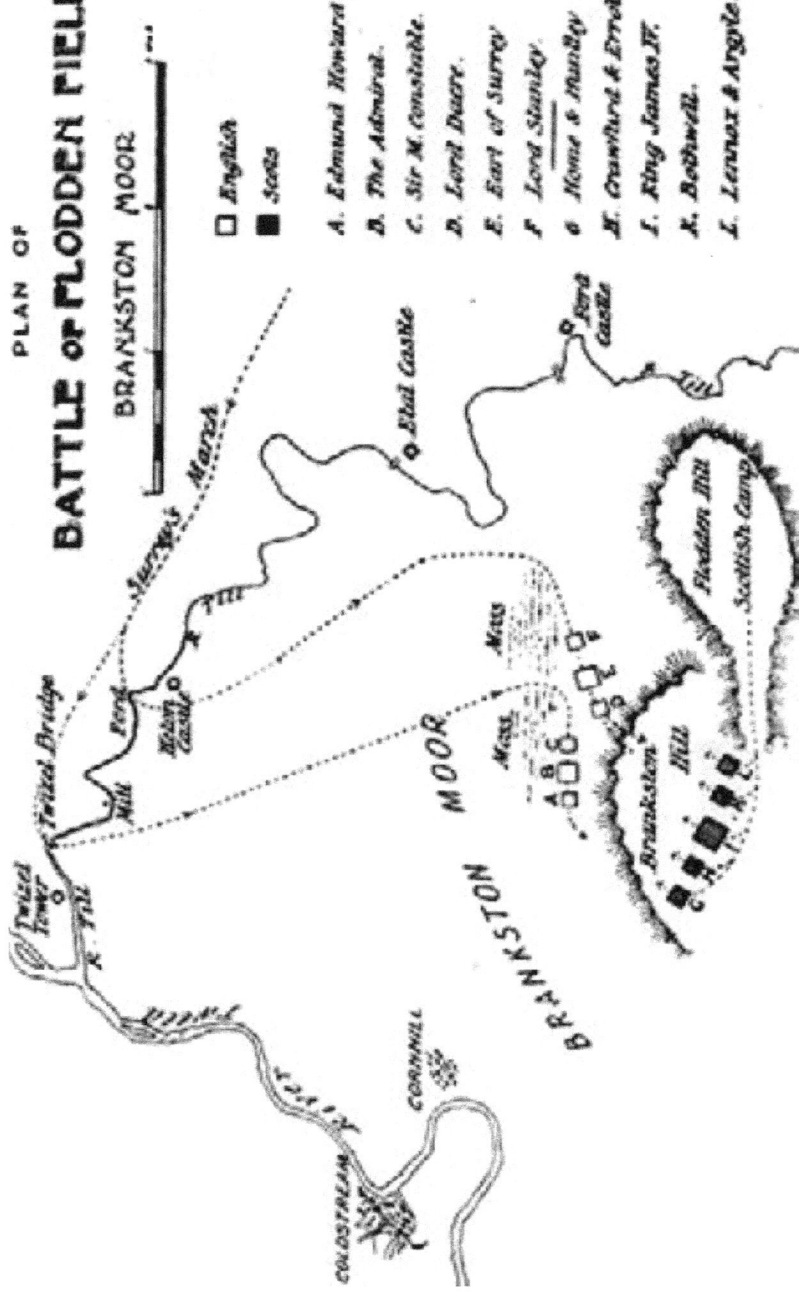

PLAN OF

BATTLE OF FLODDEN FIELD.

BRANKSTON MOOR

☐ English
■ Scots

A. Edmund Howard.
B. The Admiral.
C. Sir M. Constable.
D. Lord Dacre.
E. Earl of Surrey
F. Lord Stanley
g. Home & Huntly
H. Crawford & Errol.
I. King James IV.
K. Bothwell.
L. Lennox & Argyle.

moured men; the English bills got the better of the Scottish pikes, and the English light cavalry, admirably handled, twice saved the infantry from defeat.

Ten thousand Scots were slain, and James himself, with the head and heir of almost every noble house in Scotland around him, lay covered with ghastly wounds among the dead. He had, from some whimsical return to an obsolete practice, dismounted his men-at-arms, who, in obedience to the new fashion which counselled protection against the new-fangled bullets, were clad in the heaviest armour. Arrows fell harmlessly from them, and even bills could not cut them down with less than half a dozen strokes; but they could not fly, and the bill-men did not weary of killing. And so on Flodden Field was shown a forecast of what was to be seen later in Italy, when infantry, finding men-at-arms prostrate on the ground, hammered them to death like lobsters within their shells before they could break through their armour.

Still the lesson of Flodden to the English was mainly that bows and bills were still irresistible; and to a conservative people none could have been more welcome. Henry, who was an enthusiastic archer, had already renewed a statute of his father's prohibiting the use of the cross-bow without a licence, and he now withdrew all licences and extended the prohibition to hand-guns, (*Cal. S.P.* vol. ii, Henry VIII.). The long-bow, on the other hand, received all the encouragement that enactments and sentiment could afford it.

Henry dressed himself and his bodyguard in green, which was the archer's peculiar colour; and the Venetian ambassador Giustiniani writing in 1519 described, with but slight exaggeration, the English military forces as consisting of one hundred and fifty thousand men, whose peculiar though not exclusive weapon was the long-bow. Men-at-arms were extinct, light cavalry insignificant in number. Giustiniani, however, did not add that the archers were now more efficiently equipped than at any previous period, being provided with two stakes instead of one, and further protected by a breastplate, (*Ibid.* Vol. iii.). Nor did he notice a new weapon, the Moorish or Morris pike, which had lately come into use among the English, and had brought them a little closer to the famous infantry of the Continent.

It is, however, almost with a smile that we see Henry with undiminished satisfaction flaunting his archers in the face of Francis at the Field of Cloth of Gold, (1520). Francis on his side produced his Swiss, and gave the English an opportunity of studying the first infantry in Europe.

Fleuranges was at their head, and as his eye wandered from the scarlet and gold of the body-guard to the white and green of the other English troops, he probably felt justified in his opinion that they could not meet his own men in the open field. Henry, however, was unchangeable, and the only sign of novelty that we see at this famous pageant is a horn-shaped flag borne in the retinue of Cardinal Wolsey, the *cornette*, which was in due time to give its name to the standard-bearers of the English cavalry, (*Cal. S. P.,* Henry VIII., vol. iii.).

✦✦✦✦✦✦

At the meeting with Francis and Charles V. Henry took for his device an English archer in a green coat drawing an arrow to the head (Camden).

✦✦✦✦✦✦

Peace never endured long in those days, and in 1522 Henry was again at war with Francis, in alliance with Charles the Fifth. Again the English deficiencies became patent. In his expedition to France, which led to little result, Henry was forced to rely principally on Charles for cavalry, (*Ibid.,* vol. iii.); and when it was evident that France would require to be fought on the Scottish border also, the Earl of Surrey, who held command in the north, begged for a reinforcement of four thousand *landsknechts*. The French, he said, would certainly bring pikes with them, and the English were not accustomed to pikes, though they would soon learn from the Almains, (*Ibid*). In plain words, the English soldiers with their existing equipment were unfit to meet the French in the field. Fortunately the Duke of Albany, who was opposed to Surrey, was a coward, and little came of the alarm in the north.

But the danger seems for the moment to have aroused Henry to a sense of his backwardness, for we find in 1523 a scheme for the purchase of ten thousand eighteen foot pikes and corselets, five thousand halberds, and ten thousand hand-culverins with matches, bullet-moulds and powder-flasks complete. (In the original *lontes.* Lunt was the Scotch name for a musket-match to the end—*Cal. S. P.,* Henry VIII., vol. iii.) This is the first indication of a design to equip the army according to the best rules of the age, and, if it had been adopted, little change would have been needed for a century and a half. It is difficult to say why it was not, for at this time there are signs of an intention to take the improvement of the army seriously in hand, (*Ibid,* strength of England, 1524). But Henry changed his policy. Peace was made, (1525), and was immediately followed by a proclamation to enforce the statute for the encouragement of the long-bow and the discoun-

122

tenance of cross-bows and hand-guns. (*Ibid*). We must come down to the prolonged rejection of breech-loading artillery by the country in our own day before we can find a parallel to such perversity.

Nevertheless, in spite of all Henry's efforts firearms seem to have taken some hold on England, and particularly on London. In the general alarm that followed the insurrection known as the Pilgrimage of Grace, the King relied principally on London; and in 1537 he granted a Charter of Incorporation to the Artillery Company of the city, an association formed for the improved training of the citizens in weapons of volley, which term included hand-guns and cross-bows as well as the long-bow. This association survives as the Honourable Artillery Company. Again, at the great review of the London trained-bands two years later, 1539, we find like symptoms of a change.

The old account of this pageant is of singular interest for the sight which it gives us of the most efficient soldiers in England. The force consisted of fifteen thousand picked men, all able-bodied and properly equipped, and all, except the officers, clothed in white even to their shoes. White was at once the old colour of England, the colour of the city, and the colour of the Tudors. The men paraded at Mile End, the famous drill-ground which was later to pass into a proverb, at six o'clock in the morning, and at eight moved off on their march to Westminster, in the three orthodox divisions of fore-ward, mid-ward, and rear-ward.

First came the artillery, thirteen field-pieces, with their ammunition and "gun-stones," for shot was not yet always made of metal, in carts behind them. Then came the banners of the city, and then the musketeers, five in rank, with five feet of distance between ranks; after them came the bowmen in open order, every man a bow's length, (six feet, a horse's length was reckoned at the same figure a hundred years later), from his neighbour; then followed the pikemen with their morris-pikes, "after the Almain manner," and lastly came the bills. Every one of the five divisions in each ward had its own band, its own colours, and its officers riding at its head; and it is worthy of note that the hand-guns and pikes took precedence of the bows and bills.

So they marched on in their spotless white to Westminster, where the king awaited them on a platform. As the musketeers passed him they fired volleys, for a volley was of old the salute to the living as well as to the dead, the great guns were manoeuvred and "shot off very terribly," doubtless to an accompaniment of female screams, and the force marched back through St. James' Park to the city. The review was intended as a demonstration against the menaces of foreign powers, and it had its due effect.

The danger passed away; but within four years, (1544), Henry was again in the field fighting with Charles the Fifth against the French. There is little that is worth remarking in the campaigns that followed. The English as usual took with them their bows and bills, and the archers still came off with credit. A contingent of *landsknechts* was with them, who behaved so ill as to draw upon themselves more than ordinary dislike; and indeed the palmy days of the *landsknechts* were over. One portion of the English Army alone provoked the warm admiration of Charles, namely, the Northern Horsemen. Wallop, the English commander, took justifiable pride in them, and detached them to clear the country before the Emperor on his departure. Away started the sturdy border-men on their tough little ponies, while Charles watched with all his eyes; and when he saw them breast an ascent before them and "hurl" up the hill, he cried out with honest delight, (*State Papers*, vol. ix.).

Nevertheless it must be confessed that Henry, though the eight and thirty years of his reign were perhaps the most eventful in the history of the modern art of war, did singularly little for the army. The passion for the bow, which evinced itself in repeated enactments and proclamations to the very close of his reign, and the false system of hiring mercenaries, led to a neglect of the infantry which might easily have proved disastrous. For the cavalry, though here again he was inclined to use mercenaries, he showed more care. He was much exercised by the decay of the English breed of horses, and passed three several Acts for its remedy. The wording of these throws a flood of light on our ancient troop-horse. To improve the breed it was enacted that every owner of a park should keep from two to four brood-mares not less than thirteen hands high, and that no stallions under fourteen hands should be employed for breeding; the hand to be reckoned as four inches and the measurement to be made to the withers.

From the operation of this Act the counties of Northumberland, Cumberland, and Westmoreland, the home of the Northern Horsemen, were excluded. By a subsequent Act it was ordained that all chases, forests, and commons should be driven once a year, the unlikely mares and foals slaughtered, and no stallions allowed to run free that were under fifteen hands in height. What effect these measures may have wrought I am unable to say; but the knowledge of the small stature of brood-mares can help us to a better understanding of the difficulties which beset the maintenance of an efficient cavalry. (Henry in 1519 tried to procure horses from Italy, but was informed by Alfonso of Ferrara that there, too, the breed was decayed—*Cal. S. P.* vol. iii. part i. Henry gave as much as £35, a great sum, for his own horses).

But the arm wherein Henry worked most improvement was undoubtedly the artillery. We find him at first purchasing all his guns abroad, for the most part in Flanders, and procuring his gunners also from foreign parts; but it is clear, from the number of Englishmen whose appointment to the post of gunner remains on record, that the English were rapidly learning their business from their instructors, while as early as 1514 we find Lord Darcy pleading for the employment of native gunners, (*Cal. S. P.* 1514. 4902). There is evidence too that the artilleryman's art was by no means so rare as it had been, gunners receiving no more than the ordinary soldier's pay of sixpence a day, (*Ibid* 1513. 4375). The casting of ordnance in England was less common, though there are scattered notices of English gun-founders from the beginning of the reign.

Finally, in the year 1535 John Owen began to make even the largest guns, and obviated the necessity of depending on foreign makers for artillery. In 1543, moreover, Henry induced two foreigners to settle in England, Peter Bawd and Peter van Collen, who among other improvements devised mortar-pieces of large calibre and shells to fire from them. (Stow, mortar is the German *meerthier*, sea-beast, so other pieces were called after reptiles and monsters and birds,—serpentines, dragons, basilisks, falcons, culverins, etc.). Shell, indeed, was frequently used in the campaign of 1544, and Henry was early in appreciating its advantages.

There was, however, still the difficulty of finding horses to draw the field-guns, which he seems to have attempted to overcome as early as in the third year of his reign, (1513), by some kind of registration of waggoners and teams. The drivers were to wear the white coat and red cross, and to be mustered and paid every month; and for their protection it was ordered that their paymaster should take no bribes from them beyond one penny a month from each man, a curious commentary on the financial morality of the army. Be that as it may, however, there exists no doubt that Henry the Eighth created the British gunner who, as his proud motto tells, has since worked his guns all over the world.

His zeal as an artillerist led Henry also, perhaps almost insensibly, towards the peculiar organisation for defence which was copied at a

Landsknechts

later period by the colonies, and for a short time was expanded even into an imperial system. The mounting of valuable guns entailed the necessity of maintaining a small body of trained men to keep them in order; and thus grew up the practice of stationing small independent garrisons in all the principal fortresses, which garrisons were immovably attached to their particular posts and constituted what was really a permanent force.

Thus almost at a stroke the military resources of England fell into three divisions—the standing garrisons just mentioned, the militia which could be called out in case of invasion, and the levies, nominally feudal but in reality mercenary, which were brought together for foreign service and disbanded as soon as the war was over. The attention devoted by Henry to the defence of the coast identifies his name peculiarly with certain modern strongholds, which stand on the same site and bear the same appellation as he gave them three centuries ago. Nor must it be forgotten that, though he did comparatively little for the army, Henry did very much for the navy, and perceived that the true defence of England was the maintenance of her power on the sea.

Two small points remain to be mentioned before we dismiss the most popular of English kings. A dear lover of music he took an interest in his military bands, and we find him sending all the way to Vienna, (1542), to procure kettle-drums that could be played on horseback "after the Hungarian (that is to say the Hussars') manner," together with men that could make and play them skilfully. Ten good drums and as many fifers were ordered at the same time, with advantage, as may be hoped, to the English minstrels. Lastly, Henry was the first man of whom we may authentically say that he brought the English redcoats into the field for active service. Red garded with yellow was the uniform worn by his body-guard at the siege of Boulogne, (1544); and perhaps it was right that the scarlet should have made its first appearance in the presence of such old and gallant enemies as the French.

Under the rule of his boy successor we find little change in the old order of things.

There was the usual fight with the Scotch on the border, and yet another crushing defeat, at Pinkie, (1547), of the old inveterate enemy. But hired Italian musketeers contributed not a little to the victory; and the state of the forces of the shires was most unsatisfactory. Fraudulent enlistment and desertion, doubly expensive since the payment of coat- and conduct-money had been instituted, were as common as ever, and the dishonesty of officers was never more flagrant. A stringent Act was passed to check these irregularities, with apparently the usual infinitesimal measure of success. Foreign troops were never so much employed in England, though even they complained of unjust dealing. The insurrection in the west, (1549), was suppressed principally by *landsknechts* and Italian harquebusiers, not however before they had suffered one repulse from the men of Devon, beyond doubt to the secret joy of all true Englishmen.

Nevertheless the reign saw the rise of the Gentlemen Pensioners and, more important still, the appointment of a lord-lieutenant in every county, to be responsible for the forces of the shire. The latter was no doubt a stroke in the right direction, but it did not touch the heart of the matter. The worn-out machinery which had been patched and tinkered for five centuries was not so easily to be repaired; and a new fly-wheel, though it might turn magnificently on its own axis, could not keep the other broken-down wheels in motion.

The reign of Queen Mary, (1553), brought the most important change in the military system of the country that had occurred for two centuries. The Statute of Winchester was superseded and a new Act enacted in its place. The reform, however, was in reality quite inadequate to the occasion. It provided for the supply of more modern weapons and for a new distribution, according to a new assessment, of the burdens entailed by the maintenance of a national force; but in substance the new statute was drafted on the lines of the old, and the variations were very superficial. The extinction of men-at-arms hinted at by Guistiniani is sufficiently proved by the mention of two different kinds of cavalry, "demi-lances" or "medium" horse and the light horse with which we are already acquainted; and progress in the equipment of the infantry is shown by the mention of long pikes and corselets and of harquebuses.

But alongside of these improved weapons are the familiar bows and bills; and a clause which, considering that Mary had married the heir of Spain is truly marvellous, provides that a bow shall in all cases be accepted as an efficient substitute for an arequebus. These details, however, are comparatively unimportant. The difficulty was one, not of arms, but of men; and Mary knew it. She would have formed a standing army if she had dared, but as she designed it principally for the coercion of her own subjects she ventured neither to ask for the money to establish it nor to brave the indignation that would have followed on its establishment.

Her unpopularity at the close of her reign, so strikingly in contrast with the devoted loyalty which she had enjoyed on first mounting the throne, told heavily against the efficiency, always largely dependent on sentiment, of the forces of the shire. Never children crept more unwillingly to school than the English contingent which joined the Spaniards after the Battle of St. Quentin, (1557). Never half-witted woman looked on with more helpless, impotent distraction at the robbery of her jewels than the once iron-willed Mary, when Guise marched up to Calais, (1558).

The English garrison made all the resistance that could be expected of brave men, but they were outnumbered, and the commanders asked in vain for reinforcements. The Government awoke to the danger too late; and, yet more sadly significant, the forces of the shires came unwillingly to the musters and came unarmed. Yet Mary's name is bound up with two material benefits conferred on the British soldier. The men who went to St. Quentin received eightpence a day, the sum for which her father's men had mutinied forty years before; and from this time, for two full centuries, eightpence replaces sixpence as the soldier's daily stipend.

More thoughtful too than any of the kings that came before her, she left directions in her will for the provision of a house in London, with a clear endowment of four hundred *marks* a year, "for the relief and help of poor, impotent and aged soldiers" who had suffered loss or wounds in the service of their country. For all her man's voice and masculine will, she had a woman's heart which warmed to the deserving old soldier, and whatever her demerits in the eyes of those who wear the gown, her memory may at least be cherished by those who wear the red coat.

CHAPTER 8

Disorder in the Military System

We enter now on the fateful reign of Queen Elizabeth, (1558). The condition of England at its opening after the previous years of misgovernment was most unpromising. Wrenched from its moorings by the Reformation, the country had been tossed about by a hurricane of religious fanaticism, which, working round through all points of the compass, had left her helpless and bewildered, uncertain by which course to steer or for what port to make head. Elizabeth was by political exigency rather than religious conviction a Protestant, but her great object in life was to sail, if she could, clear of the circular storm and lie outside it. The design was an impossible one, and her obstinate persistence therein went near to bring England to utter ruin, but in the extremely difficult position wherein she found herself on her accession to the throne she had much excuse for a tortuous policy.

The finance was in hopeless disorder, and the realm through long neglect virtually defenceless. There was no discipline in such forces as the country could raise; and the military stores, which her father had taken such pains to collect, appear to have perished. The French were in Scotland in considerable force, and, as the Council pointed out, France was a state military, while England was established for peace. There in reality lay the kernel of the whole matter. England was behind all Europe in military efficiency, and all Europe was keenly alive to the fact.

The situation was so desperate that heroic measures, however distasteful to the queen from their expense, were inevitable. Arms were purchased hastily in vast quantities in Flanders, the forces of the shire were called out, and Elizabeth exercised in St. James' Park with fourteen hundred men of the trained-bands, who had been equipped by the city with caliver, pike, and halberd. But up in the north, the loyalty of the troops was doubtful, and their discipline more doubtful still. Fraud again was rife among the officers. The *landsknechts* during their stay had set the fashion of extravagance in clothing, and some captains, as it was quaintly said, carried twenty to forty soldiers in their hose. Thus, though the muster-rolls of the army in Scotland showed eight thousand men for whom the queen paid wages, but five thousand were actually with the colours, and the pay of the remaining three thousand went of course into the captains' pockets. This state of things was put down with a strong hand by special Commissioners, and the little army round Leith became orderly and efficient; but corruption had sunk so deep that it had eaten its way even among the officials of the ordnance at the Tower of London.

The French, however, were in due time compelled to evacuate Scotland, (1560), and the danger in the north ceased to be pressing. There was, however, constant trouble in Ireland; and to provide the necessary troops to keep it in order, resort was made to an instrument of which we shall hear much in the years that follow, namely, the pressgang. None the less the revelations discovered by the war in Scotland prompted Cecil to require a report from the magistrates all over England as to the condition of the population and the working of the statutes enacted for national defence. The answer was by no means complimentary to the influence of the Reformation, nor encouraging in respect of military efficiency. The people, reported the magistrates, were no longer trained to the use of arms, because the gentlemen no longer set them the example.

In plain words the old system of the *fyrd*, a people in arms, was obsolete. Not one but many causes had conspired to make it so. The country was passing through a social as well as a religious revolution; old landmarks were vanishing, old customs dying out; and the loss of the old faith had become to many an excuse for disburdening themselves of every irksome duty. Again, Calais was lost, and though there were still vague hopes that it might yet be regained, England was now strictly insular and France was closed as a field of national adventure. The people had awaked to the fact that their heritage was the sea; and the life of the corsair, free, stirring, lucrative, and dangerous, appealed powerfully to a race at once adventurous and grasping, energetic and casual, bold and born gamblers.

Moreover, the national weapon, the long-bow, and the tactics that went with it, were things of the past, while the new arms were at once distasteful and costly, and in the unsettled state of the country not to be trusted in every man's hand. The whole business of war, too, was becoming difficult and elaborate, and was passing through transitions too rapid to permit it to be learned once for all. Military training no longer consisted in friendly matches at the archery butts, but in precise movements of drill and manoeuvre, unwelcome alike because their advantages were unrecognised, and because they could no longer be learned from the old masters.

The acknowledged leaders in hundred and parish and shire gave place to experts trained in foreign schools, men who swaggered about in plumed hats and velvet doublets and extravagant hose, swearing strange oaths of mingled blasphemy taught by Spanish Catholics and Lutheran *landsknechts*, and prating of *besonios* and *alferez*, of camp-masters and rote masters, of furriers and *huren-weibels*, of false brays, mines and countermines, in one long insolent crow of military superiority. Such instructors were not likely to soften the painful lesson that war had become a profession, and could no longer be tacked on as a mere appendage to the everyday life of the citizen.

Now, therefore, if ever, was the time for the establishment of a standing army in England. She was menaced by foreign enemies on all sides, and in perpetual peril of intestine insurrection. There was unceasing trouble in Ireland, and eternal anxiety on the Scottish border. The forces of the shires had been proved to be worthless, and the service was not only inefficient but unpopular; the people came unwillingly to the muster, and would gladly have paid to be relieved of the burden. Great results would have followed from the institution of a standing force; order would have been maintained at home; interposition in foreign affairs would have had redoubled weight; untold expense through unreadiness, knavery, and inefficiency would have been spared; and finally, the British Army would have grown up to be honoured as a great national possession, called into existence to stave off a great national peril, instead of to be abused as an instrument of tyranny, and to be condemned to a blighting heritage of jealousy and suspicion.

But Elizabeth would have none of such things. She refused, to her credit, to employ foreign mercenaries, and by breaking off that evil tradition did lasting good. But she was incapable of living except from hand to mouth. She hated straight dealing for its simplicity; she hated conviction for its certainty; above all she hated war for its expense. She loved her money as herself, and to these twain she would sacrifice alike the most faithful servant and the most friendly State. She was so mean and dishonest in defrauding even such troops as she employed of their due, that no one seems to have dared even to hint to her the expediency of keeping a standing army. It may be urged that this was well for the liberties of England, but, on the other hand, it went near to destroy them altogether; and, after all, a standing army did not save either James the Second of England or Louis the Sixteenth of France. The people of England, however, saw more clearly than their tricky inconstant queen, and made good her delinquencies in their own way.

The French had not long evacuated Scotland when the desperate condition of the Protestants in France, (1562), forced the Prince of Condé to offer Elizabeth Havre and Dieppe as pledges for the restoration of the lost Calais, if she would send him money and men. Elizabeth consented; and seven or eight thousand men were despatched to garrison these two ports. Five hundred of them, English and Scots, at once volunteered to cut their way into Rouen, which was closely besieged by Guise, and fell at the capture of the town, fighting desperately till they were cut down almost to a man. These volunteers should be remembered, for they cleared the ground for the foundation-stone of the British Army, English and Scots fighting side by side for the Protestant cause in a foreign land.

The remaining troops were, as was inevitable under the parsimonious rule of Elizabeth, ill-equipped and ill-provided, a miserable contrast to the armies of the Plantagenets, and a shameful example which has been followed only too faithfully since. War between France and England at once broke out in earnest, and the garrison of Havre required reinforcement. No troops of course were ready, and it was necessary to raise recruits in a hurry. The prison doors were opened; the gaols were swept clean; robbers, highwaymen, and cutpurses, the sweepings of the nation, were driven into the ranks; and a second evil precedent, companion to the press-gang, was set for the misleading of England the Unready.

None the less these poor men fought gallantly enough against the besieging French, until the plague suddenly broke out among them; and then they went down like flies. Between the 7th and 30th of June the effective strength of the garrison of Havre sank from seven thousand to three thousand men. More men were hurried across the channel to perish with them, but the waste was greater than the repair, and in another fortnight but fifteen hundred of the whole force were left. Further requests for men and arms were met by the despatch of raw boys and of all the worn-out ordnance in the Tower—"The worst of everything is thought good enough for this place," wrote the general, Lord Warwick, in the bitterness of his soul—and finally after a grand defence Havre was surrendered.

Nevertheless, little or nothing was done to make good defects in the years that followed. The dishonesty of the officers and the indiscipline of the men in Ireland was past all belief; but it was only with extreme difficulty that Elizabeth was induced to remedy the evil, which brought untold misery and oppression upon the forlorn Irish, by the simple process of paying her soldiers their wages. It was not until 1567, when the movements of Philip the Second gave the alarm of invasion, that a corps of arquebusiers, four thousand strong, was formed for the defence of the coast towns from Newcastle to Plymouth, and prizes were given for the encouragement of marksmanship with the new weapon. Even so, practice with the bow was still enjoined upon the villagers, as though no better arm could be discovered for them, (*Cal. S. P.*, Dom., Addenda, 1561-1579).

Then came the rebellion, 1569. which but narrowly missed a most serious character, of the Catholic nobility in the North. Disloyalty was widespread in Yorkshire, and it was proverbial that the Yorkshire levies would not move without pay; but Elizabeth was too economical to send the train-bands from London to nip the insurrection in the bud, and only at the last moment consented to provide money for the payment of the troops on the spot. The difficulties of the commanders were frightful. The numbers that came to muster were far short of the true complement; horsemen were hardly to be obtained by any shift, and the footmen that presented themselves came with bows and bills only, there being but sixty firearms, and not a single pike, among two thousand five hundred infantry.

The rebels, on the other hand, were very well equipped, and had a force of cavalry armed after the newest pattern of the *Reiters*. Elizabeth's commanders wrote:—

> If we had but a thousand horse with pistols and lances, five hundred pikes and as many arquebuses, we should soon despatch the matter.

But even so trifling a contingent as this could not be produced except after infinite difficulty and delay, (*Cal. S. P.*, Dom., Addenda, 1566-1579).

For all this Elizabeth was responsible; but the peril was so great that it stirred even her avaricious soul. From this year bows and bills began slowly to make way for pikes and firearms; and a manuscript treatise in the State Papers shows that the reform was brought under the immediate notice of the Royal Council. (One sentence gives a clue to Henry VIII.'s long discouragement of firearms. "Is not the safety of the country worth more than the saving of a few wild-fowl?").

An alarm of invasion by the French in the following year, 1570, led also to a general stirring of the sluggish forces of the shire. The French ambassador reported that one hundred and twenty thousand men could take the field in different parts of the country; and the muster-rolls showed the incredible total of close on six hundred thousand men. Yet when we look into these muster-rolls we find simply a list of able-bodied men and of serviceable arms in each shire without attempt at organisation. In truth, throughout the long reign of Elizabeth we feel that in military matters one effort and one only is at work, namely, in Carlyle's words, to stretch the old formula to cover the new fact, to botch and patch and strain the antiquated web woven by the Statute of Winchester and newly dyed by the Statute of Philip and Mary to some semblance of the pattern given by the armies of France and Spain.

But when we turn from the Queen to the people we perceive the energy of a very different force. The English Army indeed was not created by a sovereign or a minister; it created itself in despite of them. The superior equipment of the northern rebels over that of the forces of the queen was typical of the whole course of English military progress in the sixteenth and seventeenth centuries. The army was conceived in rebellion, born in rebellion, nurtured in rebellion. Protestantism all over Europe went hand in hand with rebellion; and Elizabeth, always irresolute and incapable of conviction, was distracted between a political preference for Protestantism and a natural abhorrence of disloyalty. For years she struggled by the most contemptible trickery to be true to both these opposing principles, and for a time, by the help of extraordinary good fortune, she attained the success which only a false woman could 'compass.

But long before she could make up her mind, the people had taken matters into their own hands, and thereby begun the creation of our present army. It was on May Day 1572, four years later than the first rising of the Low Countries against Spain, that the army took its birth from a review of Londoners before the queen at Greenwich. In the ranks that day were many captains and soldiers who had served in Scotland, Ireland, and France, and were now adrift without employment on the world. Subscriptions were raised by sympathetic Protestants in the city, and three hundred of them were organised into a company and sent to fight for the Dutch under Captain Thomas Morgan. From this beginning we must presently trace the history of the English regiments in the Low Countries to the eve of the Civil War; and for the next seventy years therefore our story must flow in two distinct streams—the slender thread that runs through England itself, and the broader flood which glides on with ever-increasing volume in the Low Countries, on the Neckar, and even in distant Pomerania. And since at every great national crisis the two streams for a time unite, the lesser tributary may be dismissed forthwith by a brief review of the progress of the military art in England to the close of the sixteenth century.

London as usual led the van of military improvement. In the year following the departure, (1573), of Morgan's company, three thousand men of the train-bands were formed into a special corps, which was mustered three times a week for exercise, and having been armed with weapons of the newest pattern was regularly drilled by experienced officers on the once famous ground at Mile End. William Shakespeare, it is evident, was one of the spectators that went from time to time to see them, and no doubt laughed his fill at the failings of the recruits. These were sometimes not a little serious. Thus one caliverman left his scouring-stick in the barrel, and accidentally shot it into the side of a comrade, whereof the comrade died; so that the whole body of calivermen gained the enjoyment of a military funeral in St. Paul's Churchyard, whither they followed the corpse with trailing pikes and solemn countenances, and at the close of the ceremony fired their pieces over the grave, (Stow).

Something therefore had at least been learned from the landsknechts, and other changes were coming fast. The old white coat and red cross seems to have disappeared abruptly at the beginning of the reign, and coats, or, as they were called, cassocks, (from the French *casaque*, the regular term for a livery-coat, facings were soon added), generally red or blue, were provided by shires and boroughs in their stead. Once, indeed, these bright hues are found condemned as too conspicuous for active service in Ireland, and some dark or sad colour, such as russet, is recommended in its stead,—a curious anticipation of our modern *khaki*, (*Cal. S. P., Dom.*—1581-1590). Again, to turn to smaller changes, the word petty captain had dropped out of use since 1563 to yield place to the title of lieutenant, and the word ensign seems to have been accepted generally at about the same time. Sergeant had been the title of the expert at drill since 1528, but in 1585 there is a distinct order that the men appointed to instruct the bands of the shires shall be called corporals, (*Cal. S. P.,* Dom.—1581-1590).

Two years later we find officers of higher rank asking for a new denomination, and proposing that they may bear the title of colonel and the officers next below them that of sergeant-major, or, as we now call it, major. It was indeed time, for the word regiment came likewise into use at the same period, and a regiment without a colonel is naught. Before the end of the century the term infantry had also passed into the language, while the flags of the infantry, from their diversity of hues, had gained the name of colours.

★★★★★★

One bitter critic avers that the expression was due to the number of low-born captains, who, having no arms to bear on their ensigns, were obliged to trust to distinctions of colour only.

★★★★★★

But far more striking than these superficial changes is the sudden deluge of military pamphlets which burst over England from the year 1587 onwards.. The earliest military treatise, so far as I have been able to discover, that was delivered to the English in the vulgar tongue is *The Ordering of Souldiours in battelray,* by Peter Whitehorn, which was published in 1560. This book produced, no doubt, some effect in its time, but it is of small import compared with those that follow. The earliest written by an Englishman, though not published until four years after his death, was the work of one William Garrard, gentleman, who had served with the King of Spain for fourteen years and died in 1587. It is a remorseless criticism of the existing English military system. The author sweeps away bows and bills in a single contemptuous sentence, and lays it down for a dogma that there are but two weapons, for the tall man the pike and for the little nimble man the arquebus. But in the matter of equipment, he notes that the English are lamentably deficient. As good an arquebus could be made in England as in any country, but the armourers had already learned to make cheap and nasty weapons for common sale to the poor men of the shire.

Again, other nations carried their powder in flasks or metal cartridges, but the English actually carried theirs loose in their pockets, ready to be kindled by the first spark or spoiled by the first shower, and in any case certain to suffer from waste. Such slovenliness, says the indignant Garrard, is fit only "for wanton skirmish before ladies"; it is impossible for such arquebusiers to attain to the desirable consummation of "a violent, speedy, and thundering discharge." The pikemen, again, instead of a light poniard carried "monstrous daggers like a cutler's shop," fitter for ornament than use. Moreover, the dress of both was open to objection. Colour was a matter of indifference, though some fine hue such as scarlet was preferable for the honour of the military profession, but all military garments should be profitable and commodious, whereas nothing could hamper the limbs more than the great bolstered and bombasted hose that were then in fashion. I cannot resist the temptation of transcribing Garrard's picture of the march of the ideal soldier, and the delicate appeal to the soldier's vanity.

> Let the pikeman march with a good grace, holding up his head gallantly, his face full of gravity and state and such as is fit for his person; and let his body be straight and as much upright as possible; and that which most important is that they have their eyes always upon their companions which are in rank with them and before them, going just one with another, and keeping perfect distance without committing the least error in pace or step. And every pace and motion with one accord and consent they ought to make at one instant of time. And in this sort all the ranks ought to go sometimes softly, sometimes fast, according to the stroke of the drum. . . . So shall they go just and even with a gallant and sumptuous pace; for by doing so they shall be esteemed, honoured and commended of the lookers on, who shall take wonderful delight to behold them.

Earlier in appearance though not earlier composed than Garrard's was a shorter work by one Barnaby Rich, which appeared in 1587, and wherein the writer had the courage to condemn the practice of emptying the gaols into the ranks; but the great military book of the year was a translation from the French of La Noue, one of the noblest and ablest of the Huguenot commanders. Though written of course for Frenchmen, the soundness of doctrine in respect of discipline and equipment and the commendations of the Spanish system were of value to all; while of still greater import to England was the impassioned advocacy of the missile tactics of the *reiters* for cavalry. But perhaps most striking of all in the light of later events is the deep note of Puritanism to which every page of the treatise is attuned. In La Noue's Huguenot regiments there were no cards, no dice, no swearing, no women, no leaving the colours for plunder or even for forage, but stern discipline at all times and public prayers morning and evening. It is difficult to suppress the conjecture that this book had been read and digested by Oliver Cromwell.

The strong opinions expressed in these books of course provoked controversy. Sir John Smyth, knight, an officer of some repute, boldly took up the cudgels on the other side, and undertook to prove even in 1591 that the archer was more formidable than the arquebusier and the arrow than the bullet, which was an argument only too welcome to old-fashioned insular Englishmen. On the other hand, he enters minutely and intelligently into points of drill and manoeuvre, condemns the bombasted hose as vehemently as Garrard himself, and prescribes a more serviceable dress for the soldier.

From him we learn our first knowledge of the manual exercise of the pike, how it should be advanced and how shouldered with comely and soldierlike grace, and how men should always step off with the right foot. From him also we obtain sound instruction for the shock attack of cavalry, and some mention of the Hungarian light horsemen, called "*ussarons*"; and from him finally we gather information of the extraordinary inefficiency even at the close of the reign of the shire-levies of England, of the neglect of the arms and the corruption of the muster-masters.

Roger Williams, whom I have already quoted, also entered the lists at this time with an account of the Spanish organisation, and combated warmly for the superiority of the lance over the pistol as the weapon of cavalry; and a translation by Sir Edward Hoby from the Spanish of Mendoza (1597) also upheld the cause of shock-action. Hard upon these followed a version of the striking work of Martin du Bellay, with its complete scheme for what we now call the short-service system; and in the same year (1598) appeared a dialogue by one Barret, which sought to close the whole controversy. A conservative gentleman who upholds bows and bills is utterly demolished by a captain who pleads for pike and musket, would abolish the shire-levies bodily as useless, and would substitute a reorganised force on the favourite model, already once adopted in France, of the Roman legion. But Barret knew his countrymen and expected little. "Such as have followed the wars," he says, "are despised of every man until a very pinch of need doth come"; and military reform then as now could not be pushed forward except under pressure of a scare of war.

So matters drifted on to the close of the sixteenth century and beyond it. The military spirit was abroad, and the military pen busy beyond precedent. The character of the old soldier became a favourite with beggars and vagabonds, and was rewarded so freely at the hands of the charitable that it was necessary to suppress the imposture by special statute. Yet in spite of all this simmering and seething nothing was done in England for the English Army. Soldiers who wished to learn their profession sought service elsewhere than with the queen; even in Ireland the value of a company sank to fifty pounds, (Collins); and the most conspicuous type of warrior that was to be found at home was the worst.

Shakespeare, who saw everything and into the heart of everything, marked these impostors and reproduced them with such genial satire, such incomparable humour, that in our delight in the dramatist we overlook the military historian. Yet he is as truly the painter of the English Army in his own day as was Marryat of the navy in later years. Falstaff the fraudulent captain, Pistol the swaggering ensign, Bardolph the rascally corporal, Nym the impostor who affects military brevity, Parolles, "the damnable both sides rogue," nay, even Fluellen, a brave and honest man but a pedant, soaked in classical affectations and seeking his model for everything in Pompey's camp—all these had their counterparts in every shire of England and were probably to be seen daily on the drill ground at the Mile End. Not in these poor pages but in Shakespeare's must the military student read the history of the Elizabethan soldier.

CHAPTER 9

Morgan's English Volunteers

The arrival of the first English volunteers, under Thomas Morgan, in the Low Countries was, as fate willed it, most happily timed to synchronise with the movement that laid the foundation of Dutch Independence. In April 1572 an audacious enterprise of the fleet of Dutch privateers under the Count de la Marck had led to the surprise and capture of the town of Brill, a success which at once fired the train of revolt in the seven provinces north of the Waal and shook the hand of Spain from town after town first in Holland and Zealand, and later in Friesland, Gelderland, Utrecht, and Overyssel.

The incident, which time was to prove so far reaching in its results, was a curious commentary on the latest phase of Elizabeth's policy. She had just reconciled herself with Alva and forbidden De la Marck's privateers to enter English ports: the sea-rover's reply was to beard Alva in his own stronghold and deal Elizabeth's friend a blow from which he never recovered. The whole island of Walcheren, excepting Middelburg, fell into the hands of the insurgents, and Alva, who was a splendid soldier, whatever his other failings, lost no time in attempting to recover the port of Flushing. By the irony of fate Morgan's volunteers arrived in the very nick of time to save it, and in the sally which brought them first face to face with the dreaded troops of Spain they made a brilliant beginning for the new British Army. Of the three hundred, fifty were killed outright in this action, the first of fifty thousand or twice fifty thousand who were to lay their bones in Holland during the next seventy years.

Morgan, having rescued Flushing, at once wrote letters to England to point out the importance of the town which he held and to beg for reinforcements. In the autumn accordingly appeared Colonel Sir Humphrey Gilbert, with a regiment, the first of many English regiments that were to enter the Dutch service, of ten companies and fourteen hundred men, raw troops under a raw leader. Morgan would have been the better commander, but he was a modest unambitious man; Gilbert, on the other hand, suffered from fatal ignorance of his own incapacity. Sir Humphrey at once launched out boldly into complicated operations which he was utterly incompetent to direct, was outwitted and outmanoeuvred, fell back on swearing when things went wrong, and not only lost his own head but completely broke the spirit of his men. The new regiment in fact behaved very far from well. Roger Williams, the ablest of Morgan's officers, wrote after Gilbert's first defeat:—

> I am to blame to judge their minds, but let me speak truth. I believe they were afraid.

He adds elsewhere a gentle but telling criticism, that lays the blame on the right shoulders:—

> A commander that enters the enemy's countries ought to know the places that he doth attempt: if not he ought to be furnished with guides.

So ignorant were even educated Englishmen of the alphabet of war. Gilbert, however, did not learn his lesson quickly. A slight success, wherein the English displayed conspicuous gallantry, heated his ambition once more to boiling-point; he essayed another adventure in the grand manner, failed utterly, and sailed home with the scanty remnant of his regiment, a sadder and wiser man.

Morgan meanwhile had gone home and raised ten more companies, with which however he could do very little. The men were not paid on their disembarkation in Holland, as William of Nassau had promised them, and they became discontented and insubordinate. Morgan naturally took their part, and the result was, that after some few petty engagements against the Spaniards, he took his departure in dudgeon and sailed with the seven hundred men that were left to him to England. He had done good work, and his name deserves to be remembered; for he was the first man who made perfect arquebusiers of the English, and the first who taught them to love the musket.

Fifty years had flown since the Spaniards had shown the way, and the English were only just beginning to follow. Roger Williams on Morgan's retirement took service with the Spaniards for a time, in order to learn his duty the better, and presently returned, without reproach, to wield the knowledge that he had gained against themselves. To such shifts were British officers reduced who wished to master their profession.

To follow the actions of sundry other corps of volunteers during the succeeding years would be tedious. I pass at once to the landing in July 1577 of a company of three hundred Englishmen under the command of John Norris, one of the first and most eminent of the new school of officers who were the fathers of our Army. He had learned his work first in Ireland, and later in France under a great disciplinarian, the Admiral Coligny. He too arrived at a critical time. A few months after his disembarkation, while he was still in garrison at Antwerp, Don John of Austria surprised the Army of the States at Gemblours, and not only defeated it but shattered it to fragments, (January 29, 1578). Six months later, (August), Don January John attempted to repeat the blow against a second. Army of the States, a heterogeneous force of English, Scotch, and Flemings, under the command of the veteran Huguenot, De la Noue. Having but fourteen thousand men against thirty thousand of the finest troops in Europe, De la Noue took up a strong position at Rymenant, near Malines, and stood on the defensive.

After trying in vain to draw him from his entrenchments Don John finally launched a desperate attack on the quarter held by the English and Scotch under Norris. Four companies of Scots bore the first brunt of the assault, but were presently reinforced, just in time, by Norris's eleven companies of English; and then the struggle became as desperate as ever was fought by British soldiers. The Spanish troops were the flower of the army, the Old Regiment, (*Tercio Viejo*), which had not its peer in Europe; but with all their magnificent training and discipline they could not carry the position. Three times they forced the British back, and three times when success seemed assured they were met by a resistance that would not be broken, and were hurled back in their turn.

The day was intensely hot, and the British, scorning all armour, fought in their shirt-sleeves, but they fought hard, and not only hard but, thanks to John Norris, in good order. Norris himself, always in the thickest of the fight, had three horses killed under him in succession, but never lost hold of his men; and at last the famous infantry of Spain drew back, beaten, and Don John abandoned the attack. It was a great day for old "*Bras de fer*" De la Noue, but a still greater for John Norris and his British. They had, by general admission, not only saved the day, but they had repulsed the most formidable troops in the world.

During the years that follow Norris and his companies were incessantly engaged, generally victorious, though once at least defeated with heavy loss; their gallant leader, though frequently wounded, reappearing always whenever work was to be done. Their highest trial was when they encountered the greatest general of the day, Alexander of Parma, and the whole Spanish Army with him, in a rearguard action, and beat them off with such persistent bravery that the French volunteers after the engagement crowded to their colours and begged to be allowed to serve under them. Norris indeed was the Moore of the sixteenth century, alike as a teacher in the camp and as a General in the field.

Nevertheless, brilliant as his service was, he could not stay the victorious advance of the Spaniards. After ten years of fighting the Dutch States had lost almost the whole of Spanish Flanders except a few large towns and the sea-coast from Dunkirk to Ostend, and still Elizabeth would not move to help the Dutch insurgents in a task, no less vital to England than to them, which lay beyond their strength. At last the assassination of William the Silent, (July 10 1584), forced her to make up her uncertain mind to the inevitable rupture with Spain. The United Provinces were in the utmost need; the strong hand of Alexander of Parma was at the throat of Antwerp, and unless its grip could be relaxed the city must inevitably fall.

The States threw themselves upon the English queen, entreating her even to make them a part of her realm, and at last, after much paltry haggling, Elizabeth consented to send them four or five thousand men, taking over the towns of Brill, Flushing, Rammekins, and Ostend as security for their obligations towards her. Elizabeth was always careful to look after the money.

This agreement being at last concluded, (1585), the press gang was at once set to work in England; four thousand men were raised and dressed in red coats, and within a fortnight after the signing of the Treaty they had crossed the North Sea, only to find that Antwerp was already in Parma's hands and that they had come too late.

★★★★★★

The pressgangs were not very scrupulous. On one occasion they took advantage of Easter Sunday to close all the church doors in London and take a thousand men from the various congregations.—*Stow.*

144

★★★★★★

Norris, however, at once took the force in hand, and was carrying on active operations with brilliant success when he was stopped by a peremptory rebuke from the Queen; the troops had been transported for the relief of Antwerp, and she would not have them employed on any other service. The States, naturally exasperated by this contemptible double-dealing, received the troops reluctantly into the cautionary towns and left them with no very good grace to take care of themselves. Elizabeth, as her nature was, had refused to send a penny of money or an ounce of supplies, and the soldiers, ill-fed, ill-clothed, and ill-lodged, began to melt away by hundreds through death and desertion.

In December, 1585. however, Robert, Earl of Leicester, was sent out as Commander-in-Chief of the forces in the Low Countries, and as he brought with him a reinforcement of cavalry, and also money sufficient to pay the arrears of the soldiers' wages, it was hoped that matters would be placed on a better footing. But it was not to be. Elizabeth was not yet in earnest in breaking with Spain, and Leicester, gathering an inkling of her intentions from her refusal to provide him with additional funds, went very unwillingly to take up his command. On arriving in Holland he found things even worse than he had anticipated. The men were in a shocking state, dying fast of cold and hunger; they had not a penny wherewith to supply themselves; and their clothing was so deficient that for very nakedness they were ashamed to appear in public. Leicester with all his faults had evidently a genuine tenderness for his unfortunate soldiers; he wrote letter after letter pressing vehemently for money, but Elizabeth would not give a farthing.

The natural consequences followed. By February, 1586, half the men were dead, and the half that remained alive were in a state of suppressed mutiny. No good officer would accept a command in the army on such terms, and the companies fell into the hands of unscrupulous swindlers who sent their men out to plunder and did not omit to take their own share, rejoicing over every soldier who died or deserted for the money that would pass into their pockets when . the long-deferred pay-day should come. There have been many sovereigns and many ministers in England who have neglected and betrayed their soldiers, but none more wantonly, wilfully, and scandalously than Elizabeth.

Nevertheless, as the spring of 1586 approached, it behoved Leicester to open a campaign of some kind. Parma was advancing along the line of the Maas, evidently bent on taking every fortified town on the river, and it was necessary if possible to check him. The Generals, however, were ill-matched; Parma easily brushed aside Leicester's feeble opposition, and having secured the line of the Maas turned next to that of the Rhine, (July 1586).

Meanwhile a large reinforcement of men, unarmed and untrained, had been sent from England; and Leicester concentrated his forces, summoning all the garrisons of the cautionary towns to join him at Arnheim. Philip Sidney came from his government at Flushing, Lord Willoughby came from Bergen-op-zoom, John Norris and his brother Henry hurried up likewise, the veteran Roger Williams joined them, and lastly, in the retinue of Lord Willoughby, came a young man of greater promise than any, named Francis Vere. The plan of operations was soon determined; since Parma could not be checked on the Rhine, he must be called away from it by a diversion in the north on the Yssel, where the Spaniards still held the towns of Doesburg and Zutphen.

All turned out as had been expected. Doesburg was easily captured, and Parma no sooner heard that Leicester was before Zutphen than he abandoned his operations on the Rhine and marched north to relieve it. Halting on the evening of the 21st of September at some distance from the town, he sent forward a convoy of supplies towards it, protected by an escort of three thousand men under the command of the Marquis of Pescayra, (the grandson of the victor of Pavia). The convoy was to start at midnight, and it was reckoned that it would be within a mile and a half of Zutphen by daybreak. Pescayra was then to halt at an appointed place, send a messenger into the town and concert arrangements with the governor for a sortie to facilitate the entrance of the convoy.

Intelligence of Parma's design was duly brought to Leicester, who, calling John Norris, ordered him to take two hundred horse and three hundred foot and lie with them in ambuscade by the road by which the convoy was expected to arrive. Norris readily picked out two hundred horse, ordered Sir William Stanley to follow them with three hundred pikemen, and before dawn of the 22nd had successfully taken up the position assigned to him. No force appears to have been detailed by Leicester to support the ambushed party, and no scouts to have been sent forward by Norris to give warning of the enemy's approach.

The morning broke with dense impenetrable fog, amid which the English could hear a distant sound of rumbling waggons and tramping men. Presently Norris was joined by all the adventurous gentlemen—Lord Essex, Lord Audley, Lord North, and many others—who were to be found in Leicester's camp: they had not been able to resist the temptation of an action, and came galloping up with their retinue at their heels to see the sport. The sounds of the approaching convoy became more distinct, but nothing could be seen till the fog suddenly rolled away and revealed straight before them the three thousand Spaniards, horse and foot, marching by their waggons in beautiful order.

The English gentlemen threw all discipline to the winds at the sight: they never dreamed of anything but a direct attack, and one and all went at once, each in his own way, to work. Young Lord Essex called on his squadron of troopers to follow him, and couching his lance flew straight upon the enemy's cavalry, overthrew the foremost man and horse, flung away his broken lance for his curtel-axe, and with his handful of men hard after him burst into a heavy Spanish column and shivered it to pieces. The routed Spaniards fled in disorder to the shelter of their musketeers, with Essex still spurring at their heels; and then Spanish discipline told. The musketeers fired a volley which brought down many of the English horses and compelled the rest to wheel about. Then the action became simply a series of furious personal combats. Sir Philip Sidney's horse was killed under him at the first charge, but he mounted another and plunged into the hottest of the fight.

Lord North, unable owing to a recent wound to draw on more than one boot, dashed in half-booted as he was and fought as busily as any. Sir William Russell swung his curtel-axe so murderously that the if Spaniards vowed he was a devil and no man. Lord Willoughby was so beset with enemies that only great good fortune and immense personal strength served to pluck him out. Sir William Stanley's horse was struck by seven bullets but found strength to carry him safe out of action. And meanwhile the drivers of the waggons had fled, and English and Spanish soldiers were tugging the heads of the teams this way and that with oaths and yells and curses; but still Spanish discipline told, and still the convoy moved slowly forward.

Again and again the Spanish horsemen shrank before the English cavaliers, but the firm ranks of the musketeers always gave them shelter, and, charge as the English might, the waggons crept on and on till they fairly entered the town. Nothing was gained by the action. The attack, if supported, might have been fatal to Pescayra, but no support could be looked for from Leicester, and there was so little intelligence in the onslaught that no one seems to have attempted even to hamstring the waggon-horses. Zutphen therefore remains no more than one of the maddest of the many mad exploits performed by English officers of cavalry, and is remembered chiefly through the death of one of the noblest of them.

Before the action, Philip Sidney had given the thigh-pieces of his armour to the Lord Marshal, Sir William Pelham; at its close he was seen riding painfully back, with the unprotected thigh shattered by a musket bullet. He lingered in agony for some days and then died. His body was brought back to England to be followed to St. Paul's Churchyard by the London train-bands and laid to rest, as befitted a good and gallant soldier, under the smoke of their volleys. (Stow says that they fired two volleys only, which I hope is incorrect. The passage, however, shows that the reason for the three volleys was already unknown to many).

Yet another scene of desperate valour was witnessed at Zutphen before the campaign came to an end. One principal protection of the town was an external sconce, (a fort or entrenchment, German *schanze*), which on a former occasion had resisted the troops of the States for a whole year, and was now carried by the English by assault. The breach was barely practicable, the footing on the treacherous sandy soil being so uncertain that the storming party could hardly mount it. Their leader, Edward Stanley, however, was not to be turned back. Dashing alone into the breach he caught the head of a Spanish soldier's pike that was thrust out against him and tried to wrench the weapon from his grasp.

Both men struggled hard for a time, while a dozen pikes were broken against Stanley's cuirass and a score of bullets whistled about his ears. At last Stanley, without quitting his hold, allowed the Spaniard to raise the pike, used the purchase so gained to help him up the wall, scrambled over the parapet and leaped down alone into the press of the enemy with his sword. His men, redoubling their efforts, hoisted each other up the breach after him and the sconce was won. Stanley, marvellous to say, escaped unhurt, and received not only warm commendation in Leicester's despatches, but a pension for life from Leicester's own pocket, for the most daring act that is recorded of the whole of that long war.

The plot of the Spanish Armada now began to thicken, and the scene must be shifted for a moment to England. In the Low Countries Parma was looking about for a port of embarkation from which to ship his men across the North Sea. He fixed upon Sluys, and in spite of a desperate resistance from a handful of gallant Englishmen, led by Roger Williams, he succeeded in capturing it after a siege of three months. At the end of 1587 Leicester resigned his command and returned to England; and in the following year all the best officers, and many of the English companies, were gathered together in the camp at Tilbury. Leicester was in chief command, with John Norris for his second, and Roger Williams among others for assistant, but these officers were not on very friendly terms with each other; and, indeed, the less said of Tilbury Camp as a whole the better.

Contemporary writers indeed aver that it was a pleasant sight to see the soldiers march in from the various shires, "with cheerful countenances, courageous words and gestures, leaping and dancing" (Stow); but such a display was a better indication of loyalty than of discipline, and sadly different from the pace, full of gravity and state, which had been enjoined by the best authorities. There was, moreover, great disorder and deformity of apparel; most of the men wore their armour very uncomely, and the whole army refused point-blank to use the headpieces issued from the Tower. Ammunition again was short, provisions were scanty, organisation was extremely defective, and the general confusion incredible.

Four thousand men who had marched, pursuant to orders, twenty miles into Tilbury, found that they must go that distance from the camp again before they could find a loaf of bread or a barrel of beer. A thousand Londoners who were likewise in the march were ordered to halt unless they could bring their own provisions with them. Leicester might safely remark that "great dilatory wants are found upon all sudden hurly-burlies," (*Cal. S. P., Dom. (1588)*), but there was no excuse for such chaos after the , incessant warnings of the past thirty years. Elizabeth must bear the chief share of the blame. The woman who in her imbecile parsimony starved the fleet that went forth to fight the Armada could not be expected to show better feeling towards the army. It was no thanks to the queen that the Spanish invasion was repelled.

I shall not follow the veterans John Norris and Lord Willoughby on their expeditions to Corunna and Brittany in the following year, (1589). Far more important to us is the rise of a great leader, and the opening of a new era in the war of the Low Countries. On Leicester's resignation of the chief command, there was appointed to succeed him a man whose name must ever be venerated in the British Army, Prince Maurice of Nassau, (born 14th November 1567), second son of William the Silent. Though but twenty years of age when selected as Governor and Commander-in-Chief of the United Provinces, he had already made up his mind that if the War of Independence were to end in victory it must be fought not, as heretofore, with a mob of irregular levies, but with a trained, disciplined, and organised army. His own natural bent lay chiefly towards mathematics, which he cultivated as a means to the mastery of military engineering, and eventually reduced to practice by so sedulous a use of the spade in all military operations as to provoke many a sneer from soldiers of a more primitive type.

But Maurice knew his own mind, and was not to be deterred by sneers. His principal assistant was his cousin, Louis William, *Stadtholder* of Friesland, an industrious student of classical antiquity with the rare faculty of adapting old systems to modern requirements. To his diligence was due the instruction of the army in drill and discipline, and to his influence must be ascribed Maurice's admiration for the *Tactics of Ælian*, (English translation of the *Tactics*, by Captain John Bingham, 1619). His new and elaborate manoeuvres also elicited the scorn of the old school of officers, but he too was not easily discouraged; and the two cousins worked hand-in-hand, the one at the broader principles, the other at the hardly less important details, of their profession, until they raised up an army which supplanted the Spanish as the model for Europe.

★★★★★★

Hear, for instance, Tavannes, whom his writings prove to have been in many respects an excellent soldier: "*Cette grande invention d'exercice pratiquée en Flandre avec leurs demi-tours à gauche et à droit—les anciens qui n'en usaient pas (! ne laissaient de combattre aussi bien ou mieux que maintenant*" (*Memoires*). Tavannes began to write in 1599-1600, and died in 1629.

★★★★★★

Not the least weighty of Maurice's reforms, (1590), was the regular payment of the men, and the stern repression of fraudulent practices among the officers. In a word, he appreciated the value of sound administration no less that of pure military skill and training in the conduct of a war.

The tactical organisation of the new army was not so perfect as, with the Spanish model before us, we might with reason have expected. The tactical unit of infantry was the company, and the regiment still consisted of an uncertain number of companies temporarily united under the command of a colonel. The composition of the companies again was uncertain. The normal strength was one hundred and thirteen men, which was later reduced to eighty, but colonels had double companies—some even double regiments—and there appears to have been no very great exactitude, probably because men could only be persuaded to serve under the captain of their choice.

The officers of a company were of course captain, lieutenant, and ensign; the non-commissioned officers included two sergeants and three corporals, as well as a "gentleman of the arms," who was responsible for the condition of the weapons. Lastly, there were two drummers, who, it should be noted, like the trumpeters in the cavalry, were not the mere signal-makers that they now are, but the men regularly employed in all communications with the enemy, and as such expected to possess not only discretion but some skill in languages. They received far higher pay than the common soldier, and if they did a tithe of that which was expected of them they were worth every penny of it.

Every company was divided into three corporalships, each of which was the peculiar care of one of the three corporals and of one of the three officers. In equipment there were at first three descriptions of arms—halberds, pikes, and muskets—of which however the halberds soon disappeared, leaving pikes and shot in equal numbers, but with an ever-growing tendency towards preponderance of shot. The normal formation of a company was in ten ranks; and the men were never less than three feet apart from each other, such open order being essential to the execution of the prescribed evolutions. To increase the front, the ranks were doubled by moving the even ranks into the intervals of the odd; to diminish the front, the files were doubled by the converse process.

★★★★★★

Perhaps the following explanation will make this clearer:— Where an English officer would now give the word "Form fours" (to convert two ranks into four), the Dutch officer would have given, "To the right hand double your files." Where the Englishman would give the word "Front" (to reconvert four ranks into two), the Dutchman would have said, "To the left hand double your ranks."

151

★★★★★★

To take ground to flank or rear every man turned to right or left or about on his own ground, and it is worth remarking that the best men were always stationed in the front rank and the next best in the tenth, and that while the captain was posted in front of his company, the lieutenant, except in a charge, remained always in the rear.

The musketeers were usually drawn up in two divisions, one on either flank of the pikes; and the problem that eternally confronted the captain was how to handle the two elements in effective combination and yet contrive never to confuse them. In action the musketeers generally moved in advance of the pikes, firing by ranks in succession, according to Pescayra's method, and filing to the rear to reload. Sometimes they were extended across the front of the pikes, but more often they kept their place on the flanks. Meanwhile the pikemen, heavily weighted by helmet, corselet, and tassets (thigh-pieces), moved stolidly on: as they drew nearer the enemy the musketeers fell back until they were first aligned with them, and then abreast of the fifth or sixth rank.

If neither side gave way, matters came to push of pike and a general charge, wherein the musketeers ceased firing and fell in with the butt, a method of fighting which was peculiarly favoured by the English. To resist cavalry the musketeers fled for shelter under the pikes, generally in considerable disorder, and the outer ranks of pikemen, lunging forward, stayed the butts of their pikes against the hollow of the left foot.

The cavalry was divided at first into lancers and carbineers, the former being fully covered with armour to the knee; but the lance, in deference to the fashion of the *Reiters*, was soon, (1599), discarded for the pistol. The carbineers carried a carbine, (its bore was of thirty bullets to the pound), with a wheel-lock, and were trained to shoot from the saddle, the ranks firing in succession according to Pescayra's system. The tactical unit was the troop or cornet, which, after many changes, was finally fixed at a strength of one hundred and twenty men, and divided, like the company, into three corporalships. Captain, lieutenant and cornet, three corporals, a trumpeter, a farrier, and a quartermaster made up the higher ranks of the troop, no such title as a sergeant appearing in the cavalry. Of artillery I shall say nothing, since the Dutch organisation was in this respect peculiar, and could not serve like that of the infantry and cavalry as a model for the English.

Concurrently with the rise of Maurice as Commander-in-Chief must be noted that of a new English General, whose name is bound up for ever with the actions of his countrymen in the Low Countries.

Francis Vere came of the old fighting stock of the Earls of Oxford. The seventh Earl had fought with the Black Prince at Creçy and Poitiers, the twelfth with King Harry at Agincourt, and succeeding holders of the title had distinguished themselves on the Lancastrian side in the Wars of the Roses. Francis, grandson of the fifteenth Earl, was born about 1560, came to Holland with Leicester in 1585, and after brilliant service at the defence of Sluys and elsewhere rose to be sergeant-major of infantry, a sure proof that he was not only a gallant man but an adept in his profession. Finally, in August 1589 he was appointed sergeant-major-general of the Queen's forces in the Low Countries, where he was joined by two gallant brothers, Horace and Robert, who worthily upheld the honour of the name.

His task, as that of every officer who had to do with such a woman as Elizabeth, was at first no easy one. His force being very small required constant reinforcement, and was accordingly strengthened by five hundred of the "very scum of the world," such being the description of recruit that Elizabeth preferred to supply. He took care, however, to procure for himself better material, and at the opening of 1591 had no fewer than eight thousand men under his command.

But as fast as he trained them into soldiers Elizabeth required their services for her own purposes, and frittered them away in petty meaningless operations in France, filling their place with some more of the very scum of the world, which could be swept out of the gaols and taverns at a moment's notice. The system was in fact that of drafting, in its most vicious form. Vere for a time bore it in silence, but at last he protested, and like all of Elizabeth's best men was soundly abused for his pains. Still the Queen knew his value well enough to withdraw not only his troops but himself from, the expedition to Cadiz, and the disastrous island-voyage to the Azores, (1596).

A far more serious difficulty was the corruption or departments and contractors at home and the vicious system of paying the men. The wages of a private at eightpence a day were reckoned for the year at £12: 13: 4, of which £4: 2: 6 was deducted for two suits of summer and winter clothing, (these stoppages were known even then by the name of "offreckonings.") £6:18:6 paid in imprests at the rate of 2s. 8d. a week, and the balance, £1: 2: 6, alone made over in money. Even in theory the allowance does not sound liberal, but in practice it was ruinous. The men drew their pay and clothing from their captains, and the captains received the money in uncertain instalments, the balance due to them being made good at the close of every six months. This in itself was wasteful, since it enabled the captain to put in his own pocket the wages of soldiers who had died or had been discharged in the interval.

But apart from this the captains frequently withheld the clothing altogether, or served out material of uncertain quality, charging the men treble the just price for the same; or again they would make their own contract for victualling the men, of course to their own profit, in lieu of paying to them the weekly 2s. 8d. which was due to them for subsistence. How widely the practice may have obtained among officers it is difficult to say, but the system was presently altered to the advantage alike of the State and the soldier by the officials in London. The officers also had their complaints, not a whit less sweeping, against those officials, and they preferred them in uncompromising terms. Such representations were not likely to meet with encouragement. Elizabeth was not friendly to soldiers, and hated to be troubled with obligations towards men who had faithfully served her.

An Act had been passed in 1593 throwing the relief of crippled or destitute soldiers on their parishes, and she could not see what more they could want. Bloody Mary had shown them compassion; not so would Good Queen Bess; she would not be pestered with the sight of the "miserable creatures." As to the complaints of officers, she had heard enough of their ways, and would take the word of the Treasurer of the Forces against theirs. Still Vere and his captains persisted, and at last the shameful truth was revealed that the Treasurer himself was the culprit, and had for years been cheating alike his Queen, her officers, and her men.

It is easy therefore to understand the relief with which the English commanders in the Low Countries must have welcomed a new treaty made in 1598, whereby Elizabeth was quitted of her engagement to furnish the United Provinces with auxiliary troops, and all English soldiers were ordered henceforth to take their pay from the States and their orders from the Dutch generals. The troops in the Low Countries were now comparatively freed from the caprices of the queen and could work in harmony with their masters. From this point therefore the English fairly enter the school of the new art of war.

Chapter 10

The Campaign of 1600

So far I have abstained from any attempt to describe the military operations of the States, or even the brilliant little enterprises of Vere himself, since his assumption of the command: but at this point, when we enter upon the palmy days of the English in Holland, it is worth while to be more precise. So far Maurice had occupied himself principally with the task of recovering the towns occupied by the Spaniards within the seven provinces, (Holland, Zealand, Utrecht, Gelderland, Overyssel, Frieland, Groningen); the States-General in the year 1600 resolved upon the bold step of carrying the war into the enemy's country. Ostend, which was held by the Queen of England, was to be the base of operations, and the design was to land a force on the Flemish coast and besiege first Nieuport, to the west of Ostend, and afterwards Dunkirk.

Maurice and Vere both thought the enterprise hazardous in the extreme, but they were overruled by the civilians. A force of twelve thousand infantry, sixteen hundred cavalry and ten guns was assembled at Flushing, and a fleet was collected to transport it to its destination. The army was organised in the three familiar divisions, vanguard, battle, and rearguard, of which the rearguard under Sir Francis Vere consisted of sixteen hundred English veterans, two thousand five hundred Frisians, two hundred and fifty of Prince Maurice's bodyguard, and ten cornets of horse, making in all four thousand five hundred men. With Vere were men whose names through themselves or through their successors were to become famous—Sir Edward Cecil, Sir Charles Fairfax, Captain Holies, and others.

In another division of the army was a regiment of Scots under Sir William Edmunds, which had recently been recruited to the high strength of one hundred and fifty men to each company. English and

Scots already loved to fight side by side.

The force embarked on the 21st of June, 1600, but being delayed by calms landed short of Nieuport, marched overland, capturing the fort of Oudenburg on the way, and on the 1st of July was before Nieuport. The Spanish commander, the Archduke Albert, no sooner heard what was going forward than he at once concentrated his army at Ghent for an immediate advance; and Maurice, who was busily preparing for the siege of Nieuport, was surprised by the sudden intelligence that his little garrison at Oudenburg had been overwhelmed, and that the Spanish forces were in full march for his camp. The situation in which he found himself was now very critical. Expecting no such movement Maurice had divided his forces round Nieuport into two parts, which were cut off from each other by the haven that runs through the town. Though dry at low water this haven was unfordable at high tide, and the bridge which was constructing across it was still unfinished. Worst of all, it was the weakest division of the force, three thousand five hundred men under Ernest of Nassau, that stood on the side of the haven nearest to the enemy; and a battle within twenty-four hours was inevitable.

The question therefore arose whether the action should be fought in dispute of the enemy's passage over a stream called the Yser leet which barred the line of his advance, or on the sandy dunes by the sea-shore, where the Spaniards would certainly seek it if the passage were successfully accomplished. Vere was for the former course, and Maurice, thinking the advice good, ordered Count Ernest's division to march straight for the bridge on the Yser leet, saying that he would shortly follow with the rest of the army.

Vere protested in vain that this was a perversion of his counsel: either the whole army must march with Count Ernest, or no part of it must move at all; for to send forward a weak division in the hope of delaying the Spanish advance was simply to court defeat. Maurice, however, stuck to his opinion, and at midnight Count Ernest marched off with his division unsupported to the bridge. He arrived too late, for the Spaniards had already secured the passage, and he therefore took up the best position that he could find, behind a dyke, to defend himself as well as he could. The first shot had hardly been fired when his men began to run. It was such a panic as has rarely been matched in the annals of war. Cavalry and infantry, Dutchmen and Scots, threw down their arms, took to their heels and fled like swine possessed of devils into the sea.

The Scotch officers of Sir William Edmunds' regiment strove to rally the fugitives, but in vain: they were cut down one after another, and the men that escaped death by lead or steel were swallowed up literally in the waves. Two thousand five hundred men, including a thousand massacred at Oudenburg, were thus lost, and Maurice had now to face his enemy with a weakened army and with his retreat barred by the haven behind him. Defeat would mean not only annihilation but the undoing of all the work of the rebellion. With superb courage he ordered his fleet of transports to sea, and staked all on the hazard of the coming battle.

Meanwhile Vere, whose division had this day the place of the vanguard, had moved at daybreak down to the bank of the haven and was waiting for the ebb-tide to cross it, when the news came that the Archduke's army was in full march along the sea-shore. As soon as the tide permitted he forded the haven with all haste, not allowing the men to strip, for, as he said, by nightfall they would have dry clothes or want none. Presently he came in sight of the enemy, ten thousand foot, sixteen hundred horse and six guns, moving along the flat sands of the sea-shore.

The space between the sea and the enclosed country was broken up into three descriptions of ground running parallel one to another; next the sea was the narrow plain of the strand between high- and low-water mark, next the strand were the broken hillocks of the sand-dunes, and between the dunes and the enclosed land ran a margin of unbroken green, called by Vere the Greenway. Vere lost no time in taking up a position at the narrowest point that he could find, distributing his division skilfully among the hillocks to repel an advance through the dunes, and posting two guns, by Maurice's order, to command the Greenway. To his right rear stood the battle or second division, one thousand strong, and in rear of the battle the third division of rather more than two thousand men. The army was thus formed in echelon of three lines with the right refused, its left resting in the sea, its right on the enclosed land.

Weak in cavalry, the Spaniards halted till the rising tide had covered all but thirty yards of the strand, and then moved the whole of their horse to the Greenway and of their infantry into the dunes. Maurice likewise withdrew his cavalry from the shore and massed it in columns on the Greenway, leaving but two troops, both of them English, still standing on the beach. For two whole hours of a beautiful summer's afternoon the two armies waited each for the other to advance, and at last, at half-past two, the Spaniards began to move. Vere, taking every possible advantage of the sandhills to protect and conceal his men, had thrust forward small parties to contest every inch of ground; and it was against the foremost of these, two and fifty English and fifty Frisians, that the first attack of five hundred of the flower of the Spanish infantry was directed. Meanwhile the Spanish cavalry moved forward along the Greenway. This cavalry, disordered by the fire of Vere's two guns and galled in flank by a detachment of his musketeers, soon gave way before the cavalry of the States; but the struggle of the infantry in the van was very severe.

The first attack of the Spanish vanguard was repulsed, but being quickly reinforced it moved forward again and the fight then became desperate. For a time the battle seems to have resolved itself into a furious contest for the possession of a single sandhill, round which, as round the two gun battery at Inkermann, both sides fought madly hand to hand, each alternately repelling and repelled, till at last this "bloody morsel," as Vere called it, was finally carried by the English.

The Archduke without delay brought up his centre in line with his vanguard, and essayed to force his way through Vere's right. The columns were met by a murderous fire from a party of musketeers which had been posted by Vere to check any such movement, and were driven back; and then the whole strength of the Spanish attack was concentrated once more upon Vere's main position. Husbanding his strength to the utmost, Vere gradually drew the whole of his English into action and fought on. So far, owing to the skill of his dispositions, little more than half of his force had been engaged, but seeing that they were likely to be overwhelmed by numbers, he sent messengers to summon his reserve of two thousand Frisian infantry, and to beg Maurice to help him with cavalry from his right.

Messenger after messenger was despatched without result. Vere went down among his few remaining men, and the little force, cheered by his presence, fought gallantly on and still held the enemy at bay. He was struck by a musket ball in the thigh and by a second in the leg, but he concealed the wounds and held his men together. Yet the expected reinforcements came not, and the English were slowly forced back, still in good order and still showing their teeth, from the dunes on to the beach, the Spaniards following after them, but afraid to press the pursuit. As the English retired, Vere's horse was shot under him and fell, pinning him helpless to the ground. Three of his officers ran up and freed him; and mounted on the crupper behind one of them, he continued calmly to direct the retreat.

Arrived on the sands he found his reserve of Frisians still halted in their original position, having never received orders to move, and with them the two troops of English horse. A charge of the cavalry, supported by two hundred infantry under Horace Vere, soon swept the Spaniards back into the dunes, and then at last Sir Francis made himself over to the surgeon, while Maurice came forward, cool and unmoved, to save the day. The Spaniards now massed two thousand infantry together for a further advance, while the English officers, weary with fighting and parched with heat and sand, exerted themselves to rally their men. The English were quickly reformed, so quickly that the Spaniards, who had sent forward a party to disperse' them, promptly withdrew it at the sight of Horace Vere returning with his two hundred men from the beach. Maurice saw the movement and exclaimed joyfully, "*Voyez les Anglais qui tournent à la charge.*"

He at once ordered up the cavalry from the right under Sir Edward Cecil; and meanwhile Horace Vere and his brother officers hastily decided that their only chance was at once to charge the two thousand Spaniards with their handful of men. They rushed desperately down upon them; the Spaniards, worn out by a long march and hard fighting, gave way, and Maurice catching the supreme moment launched Cecil's troopers into the thick of them. A second charge disposed of the Spanish horse; Maurice ordered a general advance, and the battle was won. Three thousand Spaniards were killed outright; six hundred more with all their guns and one hundred and twenty colours were captured. On the side of the States the loss fell almost wholly on the English. Of their captains eight were killed, and but two came out of the field unhurt; of the sixteen hundred men eight hundred were killed and wounded. They with the Frisians had borne the brunt of the action, and Maurice gave them credit for it. So ended the fight of Nieuport, the dying struggle of the once famous Spanish soldier, and the first great day of the new English infantry.

★★★★★★

I have followed the narrative of Sir Clements Markham (*The Fighting Veres*) in preference to that of Motley in the description of the battle, being satisfied after careful consultation of the authorities that his account is the more accurate.

★★★★★★

Next year, 1601, the Archduke Albert sought revenge for his defeat by the investment of the one stronghold of the United Provinces in

Flanders, the little fortified fishing-town of Ostend. The garrison had made itself so obnoxious to the surrounding country that the States of Flanders petitioned the archduke to stamp out the pestilent, little fortress once for all; and hence it was that in the following years the principal operations grouped themselves around the siege. The archduke's army consisted of twenty thousand men with fifty siege-guns; the garrison of barely six thousand men, half English and half Dutch, of which fifteen hundred English, all dressed in red cassocks, were a reinforcement just imported from across the sea, (July 9). Francis Vere was in supreme command and his brother Horace commanded a regiment under him.

I shall not weary the reader with details of Vere's skill and resource in improving the defences of the town, or of the incessant encounters that took place during the first weeks of the siege. The Spanish fire was so hot and the losses of the besieged so heavy that the garrison was fairly worn out with the work. Vere was dangerously wounded in the head within the first three weeks and compelled to throw up the command until restored to health, and at the close of the first month hardly a red cassock of the fifteen hundred was to be seen, every man being wounded or dead. Nevertheless, the sea being always open to the besieged, fresh men and supplies could always be poured into the town to repair the waste.

Two thousand English, for a wonder well equipped and apparelled, were the first to arrive, and were followed by a contingent, of French and Scots. They too went down with terrible rapidity. The town was but five hundred yards across, and the Spanish batteries were built within musket-shot of the defences. Hardly a house was left standing, and the garrison was compelled to burrow underground as the only refuge from the incessant rain of missiles. The winter set in with exceptional rigour, the defenders dwindled to a bare nine hundred effective men, and at Christmas Vere, in the face of foul winds and failing supplies, was compelled to resort to a feigned parley to gain time. By a fortunate change of wind four hundred men were able to enter the harbour and recruit the exhausted garrison.

So far the Spaniards had fired one hundred and sixty-three thousand cannon-shot into the town, and they now decided on a general assault. On the 7th of January, 1602, Vere received intelligence of the coming attack, and, though his force was far too weak to defend the full extent of his works, made every preparation to repel it. Firkins of ashes, barrels bristling with tenterhooks, stones, hoops, brickbats, clubs, what not, were stored on the ramparts, and at high tide the water was dammed up into the ditch. At nightfall the Spanish columns fell on the devoted town at all points. They were met by a shower of every description of missile; flaming hoops were cast round their necks, ashes flung in their eyes, brickbats hurled in their faces; and storm as they might they could gain no footing. Thrice they returned to the assault, and thrice they were beaten back, and at last they retired, sullen and furious, for the tide was rising, and on one side they could advance to the town only by a passage which was not fordable at high water. Vere opened the sluices of the ditch as they retreated, and the rush of water swept scores if not hundreds of them out to sea. The Spanish loss was two thousand men; that of the garrison did not exceed one hundred and thirty.

I shall not further follow this memorable siege. Vere and his brother Horace left the town worn almost to death in March 1602, but still the defence was maintained. Reinforcements from England came in by hundreds and by thousands, (1603-4). Rogues, vagabonds, idle, dissolute, and masterless persons were impressed impartially together with men of honesty and reputation, clapped into red or blue cassocks and shipped across to Ostend. Volunteers of noble and of humble birth, some in search of instruction, some with a thirst for excitement, hurried likewise to the siege, and Ostend became one of the sights of Europe. Governor after governor, gallant Dutchmen all of them, came to take command. Three of them were killed outright, but still the defence continued, until at last on the 13th of September 1604 the heap of ruins which marked the site of Ostend was surrendered into the generous hands of Spinola. The siege had lasted three years and ten weeks, and had cost the lives of one hundred and twenty thousand men.

Before the town fell the campaigns of Francis Vere were ended. In 1602 he accompanied Maurice to the siege of Grave, where he was once more dangerously wounded, and in the summer of 1604 he retired from the service of the States, from whom he deservedly received a pension for his life. In the very same year King James the First made a treaty with the Archdukes of the Spanish Netherlands, which left the Dutch patriots henceforth to fight their battles by themselves; but nations like the English and Scotch are not bound by the decisions of such a creature as James. The British troops not only remained in the service of the State but grew and multiplied exceedingly, and Francis Vere, who had made their service honourable and given their efforts distinction, could feel that his work was well done.

A few short years of rest closed a life that was shortened by hardship and wounds; and on the 28th of August, 1609, within four months of the signing of the truce which gave breathing time to the exhausted combatants of the Dutch war, the old soldier died peacefully in his house in London. His tomb in Westminster Abbey is admired by thousands who know not one of his actions, but surely it is no derogation to art to remember that the recumbent marble effigy, and the four noble figures that kneel around it are those not of conventional heroes, but of honest English fighting men, typical of many thousands who perished in the cause of Dutch freedom and lie buried and forgotten in the bloodstained soil of the Netherlands.

The twelve years' truce gave the English regiments a rest which, though not wholly unbroken, left some of the more daring spirits free for other adventure. The cause of the Elector Frederick, a prince less interesting to the English as the Winter King than as the husband of their favourite Princess Elizabeth, called Horace Vere and many another gallant gentleman with four thousand good soldiers into the Palatinate, (1619), where however their bravery could not avail to save them from inevitable failure. King James of course had no part in the venture; so far from moving a finger in aid of the Protestant cause in Germany, he even conspired secretly with Spain for a partition of the Netherlands, which was to be effected by the English troops in the Dutch service, the very men who had made the cause of the United Provinces their own and had carried it through the perils of Nieuport and Ostend. It is hardly surprising that such a man should, not indeed without searching of heart but without stirring a hand, have suffered Germany to drift into the Thirty Years War.

The lapse of the twelve years' truce , (1621), found a large contingent of English under the command of Sir Edward Cecil attached to the army of Prince Maurice; and three years later the final breach of England with Spain increased its number from six to twelve thousand, and in 1625 even to seventeen thousand men. It would be tedious to follow them through the operations of the ensuing campaigns; it must suffice to call attention to the rise of men who were to become famous in later days and thus bridge over by a few stepping-stones the connection of the British army with the old Dutch schools of war. The first names are those of Philip Skippon, whom we find wounded before Breda in 1625, and of Captain John Cromwell, a kinsman of the great Oliver, who was also wounded in the same action.

Coming next to the siege of Bois le Duc in 1629 we find the list far longer—Lord Doncaster, Lord Fielding, who trailed a pike in Cecil's regiment, Lord Craven, a Luttrell, a Bridgeman, a Basset, a Throgmorton, a Fleetwood, a Lambert, a second Cromwell, Thomas Fairfax, Philip Skippon, Jacob Astley, Thomas Culpeper, the veterans Balfour and Sandilands from north of the Tweed, and many more. Lastly, at the siege of Breda in 1637 we see Prince Rupert and Prince Maurice, sons of the Winter King, as forward in the trenches as any needy cadet could be, working side by side with Philip Skippon, Lord Warwick, and George Goring. Of these Skippon and Goring divided the honours of the siege.

Skippon at a post of extreme danger drove off two hundred Spaniards at push of pike with thirty English; he was struck by five bullets on helmet and corselet and at last shot through the neck, but he merely sat down for ten minutes and returned to his work until recalled by the Prince of Orange. Goring in the extreme advanced sap paid extra wages from his own pocket to any who would work with him, and remained there while two-and-twenty men were shot down round him, until at last he was compelled to retire by a bullet in the ankle. Meanwhile fresh volunteers kept pouring in— Herbert, son of Lord Herbert of Cherbury, Sir Faithful Fortescue of the King's cavalry in Ireland, Sir Charles Slingsby, with many more, and lastly Captain George Monk of Potheridge in Devon, one day to be the first colonel of the Coldstream Guards, and even now distinguished by peculiar bravery.

There they were, brave English gentlemen, all wearing the scarf of orange and blue, fighting side by side with the pupils of Francis Vere, learning their work for the days when they should be divided into Cavaliers and Roundheads and flying at each other's throats. It was a merry life enough, though with plenty of grim earnest. Before each relief marched off for the night to the trenches it drew off in *parado* (this is the first instance that I have encountered of the word parade, which is evidently of Spanish origin), to the quarters of the colonel in command, heard prayers, sang a psalm and so went to its work; but though there was a preacher to every regiment and a sermon in the colonel's tent, there was no compulsion to attend, and there were few listeners except a handful of well-disposed persons, (Hexham).

It was to be a very different matter with some of them ten years later, but that they could not foresee; and in truth we find among the gentlemen volunteers some very familiar types. One of them arrived with eighteen suits of clothes, got drunk immediately on landing and remained drunk, hiccupping "thy pot or mine," for the rest of his stay. It is not difficult to understand why this gentleman was sent to the wars. Another, Ensign Buncombe, came for a different reason; he had fallen in love with a girl, who though worthy of him was not approved of by his parents. So he too was sent out to forget her, as such foolish boys must be; and he became a great favourite and did well. But unluckily he could not forget; so one day he sat down and wrote two letters, one full of passion to his beloved, and another full of duty to his father, and having done so, addressed the passionate epistle, as is the way of such poor blundering boys, to.his father and the dutiful one to the lady.

And so it came about that some weeks later the regiment was horrified to hear that young Duncombe had shot himself; and there was an ensign the less in the Low Countries and a broken heart the more in England, sad silence at the officers' table and much morbid discussion of the incident in the ranks. It is such trifles as these that recall to us that these soldiers of old times were really living creatures of flesh and blood.

The men too were learning their business with all the elaborate exercise of musket and of pike, and familiarising themselves with the innumerable words of command and with the refinements in the execution of the same. The pikeman learned by interminable directions to handle his weapon with the better grace, and listened to such cautions as the following:—

Now at the word *Order your pikes*, you place the butt end of your pike by the outside of your right foot, your right hand holding it even with your eye and your thumb right up; then your left arm being set *akimbo* by your side you shall stand with a full body in a comely posture.

The musketeer too grasped that the minutest motion must be executed by word of command. Stray grains of powder spilled around the pan disappeared at the word Blow off your loose corns, sometimes by a puff or two sometimes by a "sudden strong blast," but always in accordance with regulation. At the word *Give fire* again he learned the supreme importance of "gently pressing the trigger without starting or winking," and soon revived the old English reputation, first won by the archers, for fine marksmanship. An eye-witness records with delight that after each shot they would lean on their rests and look for the result as coolly as though they had been so many fowlers watching for the fall of their bird. Lastly, they learned a new feat, untaught in any drill-book, with which this section may fitly be closed. Pikemen and musketeers were drawn up in line, every pike with a wisp of straw at its head, and every musket loaded with powder only; and at the word every wisp was kindled and every musket fired in rapid succession. The volley met with a stop at first, to use the words of our authority, as was perhaps natural at a first attempt, but eventually it ran well; and thus was fired before Bois le Due in the year 1629 the first *feu de joie* that is recorded of the British Army. (The capture of Wesel was the occasion of rejoicing; and the details of the description leads me to infer that the *feu de joie* was a novelty).

CHAPTER 11

The British School of War in Germany

It is now needful to turn to the second and perhaps more important school of the British Army. As in the Low Countries we found English and Scots fighting side by side, but gave to the English, as their numerical preponderance demanded, the greater share of attention, so now in the German battlefields of the Thirty Years' War we shall see them again ranked together, but must devote ourselves for the same reason to the actions of the Scots.

The North Britons seem to have found their way very quickly to the banners of Gustavus Adolphus, and to have fought with him in his earlier campaigns long before he had established himself as the champion of Protestantism. To mention but two memorable names, Sir John Hepburn and Sir Alexander Leslie had risen to high rank in his service many years before he crossed the Baltic for his marvellous campaigns in Germany. But to trace the history of the famous Scottish regiments aright, they must be briefly followed from their first departure from Scotland to take service under King Christian the Fourth of Denmark, who curiously enough forms the link that connects the two schools of Maurice of Nassau and Gustavus Adolphus.

It was in reliance on promises of subsidy from the English King Charles the First that Christian first levied an army and took the field for the Protestant cause. His plan was for a defensive campaign, but this was impossible unless his soldiers were regularly paid, which they would be, as he hoped, with English money.

Needless to say, Charles when the moment came was unable to fulfil his promise, (August 17 1626); Christian was driven to. take the offensive and was completely defeated by Tilly at Lutter. The unhappy king appealed indignantly to Charles for help, but Charles could send nothing but four English regiments which had been raised for service in the Low Countries two years before, and were now, through the prevailing maladministration in every department of English affairs, weak, disorganised and useless. Their numbers were however supplemented by the press-gang, and a body of some five thousand men, unpaid and ill-found, ripe for disease and disorder, were shipped off to the Elbe.

A little earlier than the defeat at Lutter one of the many gentlemen-adventurers in Scotland, Sir Donald Mackay, had obtained leave from King Charles to raise and transport five thousand men for King Christian's ally, the famous free lance, Count Ernest Mansfeld. It does not appear that he succeeded in recruiting even half of that number, for heavy drafts had already been made upon the centre and south of Scotland for levies. Still some two thousand men were collected by fair means or foul, and even if some of them were taken from the Tolbooth at Edinburgh, it was fitting that in a corps so famous there should be representatives from the Heart of Midlothian.

But it is certain that a goodly proportion were taken from the northern counties and in particular from the district of the Clan Mackay, and that these took the field in their national costume and so were the first organised body deserving the name of a kilted regiment. The officers, from their names and still more from their subsequent behaviour, seem to have been without exception gentlemen of birth and standing, worthy to represent their nation. Some of them probably had already experience of war; one at least, Robert Munro, the historian of the regiment, had served in the Scottish body-guard of the King of France, and had learned from sad experience the meaning of the word discipline.

★★★★★★

I was once made to stand at the Louvre Gate in Paris, being then in the King's regiment of guards passing my prenticeship, for sleeping in the morning when I ought to have been at my exercise. For punishment I was made to stand from eleven before noon to eight o'clock of the night sentry, with corselet, headpiece, braselets, being iron to the teeth, in a hot summer's day, till I was weary of my life.—*Munro's Expeditio*.

★★★★★★

The regiment sailed in divisions from Cromarty and Aberdeen and arrived at Glückstadt on the Elbe in October 1626. The winter was spent in training the men, but not without riot and brawling. The officers were constantly quarrelling, and there was so little discipline among the men that a sergeant actually fell out of the ranks when at drill to cudgel a foreign officer who had maltreated one of his comrades. Meanwhile Count Mansfeld, who had originally hired the regiment, was dead, and in March 1627 Sir Donald Mackay offered its services to the King of Denmark. Christian accordingly reviewed it, and having first inspected the ranks on parade, "drums beating, colours flying, horses neighing," saw it march past and paid it a handsome compliment. The men were then drawn, after the fashion of the *landsknechts*, into a ring, where they took the oath and listened to a rehearsal of the articles of war; and so their services began. Half of them were despatched with the English regiments to Bremen, and the remainder were stationed at Lauenburg to guard the passage of the Elbe.

After a vast deal of marching and counter-marching four companies, under Major Dunbar, were left at Boitzenburg, at the junction of the Boitze and the Elbe, while Mackay with the remaining seven was moved to Ruppin. Three days after Mackay's departure, (July, 1627), Tilly's army, ten thousand strong, marched up to Boitzenburg and prepared to push forward into Holstein. Dunbar knowing his own weakness had strengthened his defences, but eight hundred men was a small garrison against an army. On the very first night he made a successful sortie; and on the next day the Imperialist army assaulted his works at all points. The first attack was repulsed with loss of over five hundred men to the assailants.

Reinforcements were brought up; the attack was renewed and again beaten off, and finally a third and furious onslaught was made on the little band of Scots. In the midst of the fighting the ammunition of the garrison failed and its fire ceased. The Imperialists, guessing the cause, made a general rush for the walls. The Scots met them at first with showers of sand torn from the ramparts, and presently falling in with pike and butt of musket fought the Imperialists hand to hand, and after a desperate struggle drove them out with the loss of another five hundred men. Tilly then drew off and crossed the Elbe higher up, and Dunbar by Christian's order marched proudly out of Boitzenburg. This was the first engagement of Mackay's regiment, a fitting prelude to work that was to come.

★★★★★★

But poor Dunbar and his four companies were to have little part in it. Shortly after he again defied the whole of Tilly's army, and after a desperate resistance the eight hundred men were annihilated, seven or eight alone escaping to tell the tale.

★★★★★★

The headquarters of the regiment was presently moved from Ruppin to Oldenburg to hold the pass against Tilly's advance, (October), and here they too came into action. They were ill supported by their foreign comrades, for the Danes gave way, the Germans of Christian's army took to their heels, and the brunt of the engagement fell upon half the regiment of Scots. After two hours of heavy fighting they were relieved by the other half, and so the two divisions, taking turn and turn, maintained the struggle against vastly superior numbers from seven in the morning till four in the afternoon, when the enemy at last drew off owing to the darkness. The spirit shown by the Scots was superb. Ensign David Ross received a bullet in the chest; he retired for a few minutes to get the wound dressed, and returned to the fight; nor did he afterwards miss an hour's duty on the plea that he was wounded.

Hector Munro of Coull, being shot through the foot, refused to retire till he had fired away all his ammunition, and before he could do so was shot in the other foot also. Yet another, Hugh Murray, being ordered to bring away his brother's corpse under a heavy fire, swore that he would first empty his brother's bandoliers against the enemy, and was shot in the eye, though not fatally, while fulfilling his oath. Yet these were young soldiers, of so little experience that they left their reserve of ammunition exposed, and suffered heavily from the explosion of a barrel of powder. They lost sixteen officers and four hundred men that day.

That night the Danish Army retreated to Heiligenhaven, but some German *Reiters* that were attached to it were so unsteady that they speedily turned the retreat into a flight; and when the harbour was reached the cavalry crowded on to the mole to seize all the transport-vessels for themselves. Sir Donald Mackay, who was himself wounded, was not the man to suffer his regiment to be sacrificed; he calmly ordered his pikemen to advance, swept the whole of the *Reiters* into the sea, seized the nearest ship, brought others out of the roadstead and proceeded to the work of embarkation. The last boat's load shoved off surrounded by the enemy's horse, and the last of the Scots, a gallant boy named Murchison, though wounded in the head and shot through the arm, swam off to the boat under a heavy fire, only to die two days later of his injuries.

The rest of the Danish Army, thirty-five troops of horse and forty companies of foot, surrendered without a blow. Hence it is hardly surprising that, when next the Scots found themselves in quarters alongside Danish horse, there was a furious riot which cost the lives of seven or eight men before it could be suppressed. But in truth Mackay's regiment was so much weakened by its losses that both colonel and lieutenant-colonel returned perforce to Scotland to raise recruits.

I shall not follow the various small actions of the earlier part of the campaign of 1628 in Holstein, though many of them were brilliant enough. It must suffice that Scotch and English fought constantly side by side not only against the enemy, but once riotously against the Danes themselves, whom they considered to be unduly favoured in the matter of rations. In May the Imperialists moved up in force to occupy Stralsund; and the *burghers* having appealed to Christian for assistance received from him the seven companies, now reduced to eight hundred men, of Mackay's regiment.

On arrival their commanding officer at once selected the most dangerous post in the defences, as in honour bound, and for six weeks the regiment was harassed to death by exhausting duty. The men took their very meals at their posts, and Monro, who was now a major, mentions that he never once took off his clothes. They suffered heavily too from the enemy's fire, a single cannon shot strewing the walls with the brains of no fewer than fourteen men; but still they held out. At last Wallenstein came up in person, June 26, impatient at the delay, and vowed that he would take the town in three nights though it hung by a chain between heaven and earth. His first assault was hurled back by the Scots with the loss of a thousand men. But the Highlanders also had been severely punished; three officers and two hundred men had been killed outright, and seven more officers were wounded.

On the following night the attack was renewed and again repulsed, but the garrison was now compelled to open a parley in order to gain time; and the negotiations were prolonged until the arrival of a second Scottish regiment under Lord Spynie enabled the defenders to renew their defiance.

Shortly after the King of Sweden charged himself with the defence of Stralsund. Alexander Leslie, whom we shall meet again, was appointed to take the command, and Mackay's and Spynie's regiments after a final sortie were withdrawn to Copenhagen. Of Mackay's, five hundred had been killed outright in the siege, and a bare hundred only remained unwounded; in fact the regiment required virtually to be reconstructed. The work of recruiting and reorganisation occupied the winter months, at the close of which the corps, now raised to ten companies and fifteen hundred men, was honourably discharged from the service of Denmark, and free to join itself, as it presently did, to Gustavus Adolphus, (February 1630).

Its first duty was to learn the new drill and discipline introduced by the King of Sweden; and as his system was destined to be accepted later by all the armies of Europe, no better place can be found than this, when it was just brought to perfection and first taught to British soldiers, to give some brief account of it.

The infantry of Gustavus Adolphus, as of all other civilised armies at that period, was made up of pikemen and musketeers, and beyond all doubt had originally been trained and organised on the models of the Spanish and the Dutch. Enough has already been said of these to enable the reader to follow the reforms introduced by the Swedish king. First as regards weapons: the old long pike was cut down from a length of fifteen or eighteen feet to the more modest dimension of eleven feet, and the old clumsy musket with its heavy rest was replaced by a lighter weapon which could be fired from the shoulder without further support. The defensive armour of the pikeman was also reduced to back, breast, and tassets; and thus both divisions of the infantry, carrying less weight than heretofore, were enabled to move more rapidly and to accomplish longer marches without fatigue. This was a first step towards the mobility which the great soldier designed to oppose to the old-fashioned forces of mass and weight.

Next as to the tactics of infantry: Gustavus's first improvement was to reduce the old formation from ten ranks to six; his second and more important was to withdraw the musketeers from their old station in the flanks of companies, and to mass pikes and shot into separate bodies. It is abundantly evident that he looked upon the development of the fire of musketry as of the first importance in war, and to this end he sought to render the musketeers independent of the protection of the pikes. This idea led him to a curious revival of old methods, nothing less than a modification of the stakes which were seen in the hands of the English at Hastings and Agincourt, and which now took the name of hog's bristles or Swedish feathers. This, however, was a small matter compared to his improvement in the method of maintaining a continuous fire.

Pescayra's system was one which, on the face of it, was not suited to young or unsteady troops. In theory it was a very simple matter that the ranks should fire and file off to the rear in succession, but in practice the temptation to men to get the firing done as quickly as possible and to seek shelter behind the ranks of their comrades was a great deal too strong. The retirement was apt to be executed with an unseemly haste which was demoralising to the whole company, and there was no certainty that the retiring ranks, instead of resuming their place in rear, would not disappear from the field altogether.

Gustavus therefore made the ranks that had fired retire through (there were only two "orders" in the Swedish Army: *Open order* for parade, which meant six feet from man to man, outstretched hand to outstretched hand; and *Battle order*, three feet from man to man, elbow to elbow), instead of outside their companies, where, through judicious posting of officers and non-commissioned officers, any disposition to hurry could be checked by the blow of a halberd across the shins or by such other expedients as the reader's imagination may suggest. In an advance, again, he made the rear ranks move up successively through the front ranks, and in a retreat caused the front ranks to retire through the rear.

This reform was as much moral as tactical; but the next made a great stride towards modern practice. Not content with reducing ten ranks to six Gustavus on occasions would double those six into three, and by making the front rank kneel enabled the fire of all three to be delivered simultaneously. Here is seen the advantage of abolishing the old musket-rest, with which such a concentration of fire would have been impossible. Still following out his leading principle, he encouraged the use of cartridges to hasten the process of loading; and finally to perfect his work he introduced a new tactical unit, the *peloton*, called by Munro *plotton* and later naturalised among us as the platoon of musketeers, which consisted of forty-eight men, eight in rank and six in file, all of course carefully trained to the new tactics. Yet with all these changes the drill was of the simplest; if men could turn right, left, and about, and double their ranks and files, that was sufficient.

In the matter of pure organisation Gustavus again improved upon all existing systems. First he made the companies of uniform strength, one hundred and twenty-six men, distributed into twenty-one *rots* or files, and six corporalships. A corporalship of pikes consisted of three files, and of musketeers of four files; and to every file was appointed a *rottmeister* or leader, who stood in the front, and an *unter-rottmeister* or sub-leader, who stood in the rear rank.

★★★★★★

A file in those days consisted, of course, of six men, not as now of two. So a corporalship of pikes would be eighteen, and of musketeers twenty-four men.

The *rottmeisters* were fifteen in number, the six corporals bringing up the total to the necessary twenty-one.

★★★★★★

Both of these received higher pay than the private soldier. Two sergeants, four under-sergeants and a quartermaster-sergeant completed the strength of non-commissioned officers, while three pipers and as many drums made music for all. Moreover each company carried a kind of reserve with it in the shape of eighteen supernumerary men who bore the name of *passe-volans*, the old slang term for fictitious soldiers since the days of Hawkwood, and were allowed to the captain as free men, unmustered. The officers of course were as usual captain, lieutenant, and ensign.

Eight such companies constituted a regiment, which was thus one thousand and eight men strong, with a colonel, lieutenant-colonel, and major over all. The regimental staff included many officials borrowed from the landsknechts' model for the trial and punishment of offenders, and for a complete novelty, four surgeons. The provision of medical aid had formerly been left to the captains, and it is to Gustavus that we owe the first example of a sounder medical organisation.

Four companies or half of such a regiment were called either a squadron or by the Italian name *battaglia*, to which must be traced our modern word battalion. Two such regiments were called a brigade, which marks the latest advance in organisation made by Gustavus. Maurice of Nassau had been before him in the formation of brigades but had not reduced them to uniform strength. The Swedish brigades had a stereotyped formation for battle, and were called after the colour of their standards, the white, the blue, the yellow, and finally the green, better known as the Scots Brigade, which is that wherein we are chiefly interested.

Passing next to the cavalry, the marks of Gustavus's reforming hand are not less evident. The force at large was divided into cuirassiers and dragoons, Of these the latter, who were armed with muskets and were simply mounted infantry, may be dismissed without further observation. The cuirassiers, except outwardly, bore a strong resemblance to the *Reiters*, for, though stripped of all defensive armour except cuirass and helmet, they still carried two pistols as well as the sword. Gustavus, however, here as with the infantry, took a line of his own. He began

173

by reducing the depth of the ranks from the bottomless profundity of the *Reiters* to three or at most four; and though he still opened his attack with the pistol and so far adhered to missile tactics he to a considerable extent combined with them the action by shock. As in the infantry, it was Pescayra's system that he wished to supersede. The *Reiters*, as we know by the testimony of many eye-witnesses, were often so anxious to go to the rear and reload that they fired their pistols at absurd ranges, sometimes indeed hardly waiting to fire before they turned about.

Unable to apply to cavalry the system which he had adopted for the infantry, and failing in common with all his contemporaries to grasp the principle that, since a horse has four legs and a man two, the evolutions of horse and foot must be fundamentally different, Gustavus none the less determined that his *cuirassiers* should at all events come to close quarters with their enemy. He therefore trained them not to fire till they could see the white of their opponents' eyes, and having fired to strike in with the sword.

Hence he has the credit, which is not wholly undeserved, of having restored shock-action, and is said to have made his cavalry charge at the gallop; but the first statement is misleading, and the second in the face of contemporary accounts incredible. In the first place, the sword is a singularly ineffective weapon against mailed men, and a true restorer of shock-action would almost certainly have reverted to the lance. In the second place, mounted men who open their attack with pistols will infallibly check their horses at the moment of firing in order to ensure greater accuracy of aim. Lastly, Gustavus's favourite plan for the attack of cavalry was to intersperse his squadrons with platoons of musketeers, which advanced with them within close range , (Monro, vol. ii.), and fired a volley into the enemy's horse.

This preliminary over, the *cuirassiers* advanced, fired their pistols, fell in with the sword, and retired; by which time the musketeers had reloaded and were ready with another volley. Close range of the musket of those days would not have allowed space for a body of horse to gather way for a shock-attack in the modern sense, and it is therefore more than doubtful whether the Swedish squadrons charged at higher speed than the trot. Gustavus's system was in fact simply a revival of Edward the First's at Falkirk, which had already been developed with great success by Pescayra at Pavia. Nevertheless, by reducing the depth of squadrons and insisting that his men should come to close quarters, Gustavus unquestionably did very much for the improvement of cavalry.

★★★★★★

Stress has been laid upon the fact that Gustavus always led the cavalry in person. Doubtless he was fond of his Horse, but since at that period cavalry was always stationed in the wings, and the right wing was the post of honour, this does not count for very much.

★★★★★★

They were called after their inventor by the name of "Sandy's stoups," and were used by the Scots at the Battle of Newburn in 1640.

★★★★★★

Most remarkable of all were his reforms in the matter of artillery. Profoundly impressed by the power of field-guns he spared no effort to make them lighter and more mobile, so as to be at once easily manoeuvred and capable of transport in larger numbers. Here again Maurice had been before him, not without success, but Gustavus possessed in the person of a Scotch gentleman, Sir Alexander Hamilton, an artillerist of wider views than lay to the hand of the great Dutch soldier. Hamilton's first experiment was to make leathern guns, strengthened by hoops of metal and with apparently a core of tin, which could easily be carried on a pony's back or stacked away by the dozen in a waggon.

★★★★★★

Gustavus used them frequently in his earlier campaigns but discarded them at latest after the Battle of Breitenfeld, finding that their life did not extend beyond ten or a dozen rounds. He then fell back on light two-pounders and four-pounders, which required few horses for draught, and could be loaded and fired by a skilful crew more rapidly even than a musket. A few such guns were attached to each regiment and called regimental pieces; and very effective they were presently found to be.

Further, Gustavus was a consummate engineer, as fond of the spade as Maurice himself, and a past master of field-fortification. On stepping ashore in Germany he first fell on his knees and prayed, and then picking up a spade began to dig with his own hands. This, it may here be mentioned once for all, was the one point in his system which the Scots could not endure; they always grumbled when called upon to use the spade, and in spite of the king's occasional reproaches, always made less progress with field-works in a given time than any other corps in the army.

Lastly, to turn to broader principles, the great innovation of Gustavus, visible in all his reforms, was to match mobility against the old system of weight. He never massed his troops in unwieldy bodies, but distributed them in smaller and more flexible divisions, allowing plenty of space for facility of manoeuvre. His order of battle was that which was customary in his time, consisting of two lines with infantry in the centre and cavalry on the flanks; but he always allowed three hundred yards of distance between the first and second line, and erected the practice of keeping a reserve, which had been intermittently observed for centuries, into an established principle. Again, he carefully studied the effective combination of the three arms with a thoroughness unknown since the days of Zizca, supplying artillery to his infantry, and supporting impartially horse with foot and foot with horse. Finally, as the backbone of all, he enforced with a strictness that had never been seen before him the observance of discipline.

Such was the army and such the general to which Mackay's regiment now joined itself. In June 1630 it embarked for Germany as part of the thirteen thousand men which formed the Swedish army, half of the companies at Elfsknaben, the remainder under Munro at Pillau. The latter detachment was wrecked off Rügenwalde, which was held by the Imperialists, and lost everything; but having made shift to obtain arms calmly attacked the Imperial garrison and captured the town—as daring a feat of arms as ever was done by Scotsmen. After several small engagements Monro rejoined his headquarters at Stettin, and in January 1631 Gustavus, who boasted with justice that his army was as effective for a winter's as for a summer's campaign, invaded Brandenburg and marched for the Oder. The Scotch were organised into the famous Scots Brigade, consisting of four picked regiments—Hepburn's, Mackay's, Stargate's, and Lumsden's, the whole under the command of Sir John Hepburn.

We must pass over the operations in Brandenburg, where the Scots Brigade distinguished itself repeatedly, and come forthwith to Saxony, whither Gustavus had been called from the Oder by Tilly's advance upon Magdeburg, (May). Arriving too late to save the unhappy city he entrenched himself at Werben, at the junction of the Elbe and the Havel, and gave the world a first notable example of his skill as an engineer. Tilly, having lost six thousand men in the vain attempt to storm the entrenchments, invaded Saxony, whither Gustavus at once followed him and offered him battle on the plain of Leipsic.

On the 7th of September Tilly took up his position facing north, on a low line of heights running from the village of Breitenfeld on the west to that of Seehausen on the east. His army was drawn up in a single line. On each wing as usual was posted the cavalry, seven regiments under Pappenheim on the left, seven more under Furstenburg on the right, all drawn up in the dense columns beloved of Charles the Fifth. In the centre was Tilly himself, with eighteen regiments of infantry, his famous Walloons among them, massed together in the old heavy Spanish formation. On the heights above him were his guns. The whole force numbered forty thousand men, and their general was a man who, though seventy years of age, had never lost a battle.

On the other side the armies of Gustavus and of his allies the Saxons were drawn up in two lines. On the left were the Saxons, fourteen thousand strong, and on the right, with which alone we need concern ourselves, the Swedes. In touch with the Saxon right, the Swedish left under Field-Marshal Horn was made up, both in the first and second lines, of six regiments of horse, with four platoons of musketeers between each regiment. The right wing under Gustavus himself was similarly composed, (Sept. 7). In the centre the first line was made up of four half brigades of foot, supported by a regiment of cavalry and eight platoons of Scots; and the second line of three brigades, of which Hepburn's was one. In rear of both lines was a reserve of cavalry, and in the extreme rear a further reserve, the first ever seen, of artillery.

The battle opened as usual with a duel of artillery, which was continued from noon till half-past two, the Swedish guns, more numerous and better served than Tilly's, firing three shots to the enemy's one. Then Pappenheim, on Tilly's left, lost patience, and setting his cavalry in motion without orders came down upon the Swedish right. He was met by biting volleys from the platoons of musketeers and charges from the *cuirassiers* at their side; his men shrank from the fire, and edging leftward across the front of Gustavus's wing swept down towards its rear. General Bauer, in command of the reserve cavalry of the first line, at once moved out and broke into them; and the whole Swedish right coming into action drove back Pappenheim's horse, after a hard struggle, in disorder. Gustavus checked the pursuit, for Tilly had pushed forward a regiment of infantry in support of Pappenheim, and turning all his force on this unhappy corps annihilated it.

On the Imperialists' left Furstenburg, following Pappenheim's example, had also charged, and had driven the entire Saxon Army before him like chaff before the wind, (Tallard fatally repeated this independent formation of two armies at Blenheim). He followed them in hot pursuit; and had Tilly at once advanced with his centre against Field-Marshal Horn, the situation of the Swedes would have been critical, for their left was now completely uncovered.

But owing to the faulty disposition of his artillery Tilly could not advance directly without putting his guns out of action, and he therefore followed in the track of Furstenburg to turn Horn's left flank. The delay gave Horn time to make dispositions to meet the attack. Hepburn's brigade came quickly up with another brigade, (Sept. 7), m support, and the Scots after one volley charged the hostile infantry with the pike and routed it completely. Gustavus meanwhile had again advanced with his cavalry on the right, and sweeping down on the flank of Tilly's battery captured all his guns and turned them against himself. The battle was virtually over, but four splendid old Walloon regiments stood firm to the last, and though reduced to but six hundred men retreated at nightfall in good order.

The victory was crushing; and yet of all the Swedish infantry two brigades alone had been engaged, and of these the Scots had done the greater share of the work. The battle marks the death-day of the old dense formations and the triumph of mobility over weight, and is therefore of particular interest to a nation whose strength is to fight in line.

From Leipsic Gustavus marched for the Main, where the Scots were as usual put forward for every desperate service, and held his winter court at Mainz. In the spring of the following year, (1632), he marched down to the line of the Danube with forty thousand men, forced the passage of the Lech in the teeth of Tilly's army, entered Bavaria and by May was at Munich. Then hearing that the towns on the Danube in his rear were threatened he turned back to Donau-wörth, whence he was called away by the movements of Wallenstein in Saxony to Nürnberg. Such marching had not been since the days of Zizca. He now turned Nürnberg, as he had turned Werben in the previous year, into a vast entrenched camp; for he had now but eighteen thousand men against Wallenstein's seventy thousand, and it behoved him to make the most of his position.

Wallenstein, however, without risking an engagement, took the simpler course of making also an entrenched camp, cutting off Gustavus's supplies from the Rhine and Danube, and reducing him by starvation. Reinforcements came to the Swedes, which raised their army to five-and-thirty thousand men; Wallenstein allowed them to pass in unmolested to consume the provisions the quicker.

The pinch of hunger began to make itself felt in the Swedish camp, pestilence raged among the unhappy troops, and at last Gustavus in desperation launched his army in a vain assault upon Wallenstein's entrenchments. For twelve hours his men swarmed up the rugged and broken hill with desperate courage, three times obtaining a momentary footing and as often beaten back. The cannonade was kept up all night, and it was not till ten o'clock on the following morning that the Swedes retreated, leaving four thousand dead behind them. The Scots Brigade suffered terribly. Monro, out of a detachment of five hundred men, lost two hundred killed alone, besides wounded and missing. His lieutenant-colonel who relieved him at night brought back but thirty men next morning. Other corps had lost hardly less heavily, and Gustavus, foiled for once, retreated to Neustadt, leaving one-third of his force dead around Nürnberg.

Sir John Hepburn, in consequence of a quarrel with the Swedish king, now took leave of him and entered the service of France; and the Scots Brigade, weakened to a mere shadow, was left behind at Dunkerswald to await reinforcements, while Gustavus marched away to his last battlefield at Lützen. We need follow the fortunes of the Brigade little further. The famous regiments, together with the other Scots and English in the Swedish service, now some thirteen thousand men, did abundance of hard and gallant work before the close of the war.

The ranks of Mackay's regiment were again swelled to twelve companies and fifteen hundred men, but at Nordlingen, August 26, 1634, it was almost annihilated, and emerged with the strength of a single company only. Times had changed, and discipline had decayed since the death of Gustavus; and in 1635, on the alliance of France with Sweden, and the outbreak of war between France and Spain, the fragments of all the Scotch regiments were merged together, and passed into the service of France under the command of the veteran Sir John Hepburn as the Regiment d'Hebron.

There for a short period let us leave it, wrangling with Regiment Picardie for precedence, claiming, on the ground that some officers of the Scottish Guard had joined it, to be the oldest regiment in the world, and earning the nickname of Pontius Pilate's guards.

★★★★★★

As I believe that this pretension is still advanced by patriotic North Britons, it is as well to say that it is preposterous. The true Scottish Guard enjoyed an independent existence till the

179

Revolution, and to claim its privileges for Hepburn's regiment is as absurd as though a corps raised tomorrow, and officered by half a dozen gentlemen of the Grenadier Guards, should claim precedence of all British infantry.

★★★★★★

Hepburn commanded it for but one year, for he fell at its head at the siege of Saverne, 1636, but it fought through many actions and many sieges, the battle of Rocroi not the least of them, before it returned to the British Isles.

CHAPTER 12

Buckingham's Military Mismanagement

Once more we return to England and take up the thread of the army's history within the kingdom. Of the reign of James the First there is little to be recorded except that at its very outset the Statute of Philip and Mary for the regulation of the Militia was repealed, and the military organisation of the country based once more on the Statute of Winchester. James was not fond of soldiers, and military progress was not to be expected of such a man. Enough has already been seen of his methods through his dealings with the Low Countries, and there is no occasion to dwell longer on the first British king of the House of Stuart.

Charles the First was more ambitious, and sufficiently proud of the English soldier to preserve the ancient English drum-march, (Dalton, vol. i.). Soon after the final breach with Spain, 1625, he imbibed from Buckingham the idea of a raid on the Spanish coast after the Elizabethan model, which eventually took shape in the expedition to Cadiz. Of all the countless mismanaged enterprises in our history this seems on the whole to have been the very worst. There was abundance of trained soldiers in England who had learned their duty in the Low Countries; and Edward Cecil, he whom we saw some few years back in command of the cavalry at Nieuport, begged that liberal offers might be made to induce them to serve.

Officers again could be procured from the Low Countries, and therefore there should have been no difficulty in organising an excellent body of men. In the matter of arms, however, though English cannon was highly esteemed, Charles was forced to purchase what he needed from Holland, which was a sad reflection on our national enterprise. Accordingly over a hundred officers were recalled from Holland; and two thousand recruits were collected, to be sent in exchange for the same number of veterans from the Dutch service. Eight thousand men were then pressed for service in various parts of England, and the whole of them poured, without the least preparation to receive them, into Plymouth, where they gained for themselves the name of the plagues of England. Sir John Ogle, a veteran who had served for years with Francis Vere, eyed these recruits narrowly for a time, old, lame, sick and destitute men for the most part, and reflected how without stores, clothes, or money he could possibly convert them into soldiers. Then taking his resolution he threw up his command and took refuge in the Church.

Very soon another difficulty arose. The States-General firmly refused to accept two thousand raw men in exchange for veterans, and shipped the unhappy recruits back to England. They too were turned into Plymouth and made confusion worse confounded. Then the arms arrived from Holland, and there was no money to pay men to unload them. The port became a chaos. Buckingham had already shuffled out of the chief command and saddled it on Cecil, and the unfortunate man, good soldier though he was, was driven to his wit's end to cope with his task. His tried officers from Holland were displaced to make room for Buckingham's favourites, who were absolutely useless; and yet he was expected to clothe, arm, train, discipline, and organise ten thousand raw, naked men, work out every detail of a difficult and complicated expedition, and make every provision for it, all without help, without encouragement, and without money. Cash indeed was so scarce that the king could not afford to pay the expenses of his own journey to Plymouth.

Under such conditions it is hardly surprising that the enterprise was a disastrous failure. A few butts of liquor left by the Spaniards outside Cadiz sufficed to set the whole force fighting with its own officers, and after weary weeks at sea, aggravated by heavy weather and by pestilence, the result of bad stores, Cecil and the remains of his ten regiments returned home in misery and shame. (See Dalton *Life of Cecil*).

A similar enterprise under Lord Willoughby in the following year, 1626, failed in the same way for precisely the same reasons; but Buckingham, still unshaken in his confidence, led a third and a fourth expedition to Rochelle with equal disaster and equal disgrace. The captains had no more control over their men than over a herd of deer,

(Ward, *Animadversions of Warre*). At last, at the outset of a fifth expedition, which promised similar failure, the dagger of Lieutenant Felton, a melancholy man embittered by deprivation of his pay, put an end to Buckingham and to all his follies. On the whole he had not treated the soldiers worse than Elizabeth, but a man of Elizabeth's stamp was more than could be borne with.

Nevertheless, amid all these failures there were still plenty of men in England who had the welfare of the military profession at heart. Foremost among them was the veteran Edward Cecil, now Lord Wimbledon, who strove hard to do something for the defence of the principal ports, for the training of the nation at large, and in particular for the encouragement of cavalry. The mounted service had become strangely unpopular with the English at this time, whether because the eternal sieges of the Dutch war afforded it less opportunity of distinction, or because missile tactics had lowered it from its former proud station, it is difficult to say. Certain it is that officers of infantry, and notably Monro, never lost an opportunity of girding at horsemen as fitted only to run away, and as preferring to be mounted only that they might run away the faster.

But Cecil, though in this respect unique, was by no means the only man who made his voice heard. Veteran after veteran took pen in hand and wrote of the discipline of Maurice of Nassau and, as time went on, of the system of Gustavus Adolphus; while on the other hand one ingenious gentleman, still jealous of the old national weapon, invented what he called a "double-arm," which combined the pike and the bow, the bow-staff being attached to the shaft of the pike by a vice which could be traversed on a hinge. Strange to say this belated weapon was not ill-received in military circles and found commendation even among Scotsmen. (See *Pallas Armata*, Sir T. Kellie, 1627, the first who introduced the system of drilling by numbers, he talks as glibly of odd and even numbers as a modern drill sergeant).

On one important point, however, there was a general consensus of opinion, namely that the condition of the English militia was disgraceful, its system hopelessly inefficient and the corruption of its administration a scandal. The trained bands were hardly called out once in five years for exercise; few men knew how even to load their muskets, and the majority were afraid to fire a shot except in salute of the colours, not daring to fire a bullet from want of practice, (Barriffe and Ward).

The Londoners, as usual, alone made a favourable exception to the general rule. The real root of the evil was presently to be laid bare. The disputes between Charles the First and his subjects were assuming daily an acuter form, until at last they came to a head in the Scotch rebellion of 1639. It was imperative to raise an English force forthwith and move it up to the Border. Charles, as usual in the last stage of impecuniosity, thought to save money by an exercise of old feudal rights, and summoned every peer with his retinue to attend him in person as his principal force of cavalry.

It was a piece of tactless folly whereof none but a Stuart would have been guilty: the peers came in some numbers as they were bid, but they did not conceal their resentment against such proceedings. The foot were levied as usual by writ to the lord-lieutenant with the help of the press-gang, they behaved abominably on their march to the rendezvous, and on arrival were found to be utterly inefficient. Their arms were of all sorts, sizes, and calibres, and the men were so careless in the handling of them that hardly a tent in the camp, not even the king's, escaped perforation by stray bullets. In other respects the organisation was equally deficient; no provision had been made for the supply of victuals and forage; and altogether it was fortunate that the force escaped, through the pacification of Berwick, an engagement with the veterans from the Swedish service under old Alexander Leslie that composed a large portion of the Scottish army.

The following year, 1640, saw the war renewed. This. time the farce of calling out a feudal body of horse was not repeated, but unexpected difficulties were encountered in raising the levies of foot. In 1639 the infantry had been drawn chiefly from the northern counties, where the tradition of eternal feuds with the Scots made men not altogether averse to a march to the Border. But in 1640 the trained bands of the southern counties were called upon, and they had no such feeling. It is possible that unusual rigour was employed in the process of impressment, for the authorities had been warned, after experience of the previous year, to allow no captains to play the Falstaff with their recruits. Be that as it may, the recalcitrance of the new levies was startling.

From county after county came complaints of riot and disorder. The Wiltshire men seized the opportunity to live by robbery and plunder; the Dorsetshire men murdered an officer who had corrected a drummer for flagrant insubordination; in Suffolk the recruits threatened to murder the deputy-lieutenant; in London, Kent, Surrey, and half a dozen more counties the resistance to service was equally determined; and when finally in July four thousand men reached the rendezvous at Selby, old Sir Jacob Astley could only designate them as the arch-knaves of the country. Money being of course very scarce, the men were ill-clothed and ill-found, and their numbers were soon thinned by systematic desertion. A new difficulty cropped up in the matter of discipline. Lord Conway, who commanded the horse, had executed a man for mutiny; he now found that his action was illegal and that he required the royal pardon. If, he wrote, the lawyers are right and martial law is impossible in England, it would be best to break up the army forthwith: to hand men over to the civil power is to deliver them to the lawyers, and experience of the ship-money has shown what support could be expected from them.

There, in fact, lay the kernel of the whole matter; indiscipline was not only rife in the ranks but widespread throughout the nation. From long carelessness and neglect the organisation of the country for defence by land and sea had become not only obsolete but impossible and absurd. For centuries the old vessel had been patched and tinkered and filed and riveted, occasionally by statute, more often by royal authority only, but chiefly by mere habit and custom. But now that the reaction which had established the new monarchy was over, and men, stirred by a counter-reaction, subjected the military system to the fierce haat of constitutional tests, the whole fabric fell asunder in an instant, and brought the new monarchy down headlong in its fall. The story is so instructive to a nation which has not yet given its standing army a permanent statutory existence, that it is worth while very briefly to trace the progress of the catastrophe.

According to ancient practice, the various shires were called upon to provide their levies for the Scotch war with coat-money and with conduct-money to pay their expenses till they had passed the borders of the county, from which moment they passed into the king's pay. The writs to the lord-lieutenants distinctly stated that these charges would be refunded from the Royal Exchequer, and though the chronic emptiness of the Royal Exchequer might diminish the value of the pledge, the form of the writ was distinctly consonant with custom and precedent.

Many of the county gentlemen, however, refused to pay this coat- and conduct-money; they had been encouraged by the attacks made on military charges in the Short Parliament; and the Crown, aware of the general opposition to all its doings, did not venture to prosecute. Another incident raised the general question of military obligations in an acuter form. In August 1640, Charles, sadly hampered by the general objections to military service on any terms, fell back on the old system of issuing Commissions of Array to the lord-lieutenants and sheriffs. In themselves Commissions of Array, especially when addressed to these particular officers, were nothing extraordinary; they had been in use to the reign of Queen Mary, and though more or less superseded by the appointment of lord-lieutenants, were by implication sanctioned by a statute of Henry the Fourth.

Now, however, these Commissions at once raised a storm. The deputy-lieutenants of Devon promptly approached the Council with an awkward dilemma. To which service, they asked, were the gentry to attach themselves, to the trained bands or to the feudal service implied in the Commissions of Array; since both were equally enjoined by proclamation? The Council answered that the service in the trained bands must be personal, and the feudal obligation satisfied by deputy or by pecuniary composition; in other words, if the gentry halted between two services, they could not go wrong in performing both.

A second question from the deputy-lieutenants was still more searching: how were the bands levied under the Commissions to be paid? The reply of the Council pointed out that the laws and customs of the realm required every man, in the event of invasion, to serve for the common defence at his own charge. Here Charles was strictly within his rights; and the plea of invasion was sound, since the Scots had actually passed the Tweed. Parliament, however, seized hold of the Commissions of Array, and after innumerable arguments as to their illegality, took final refuge under the Petition of Right. Stripped of all redundant phrases, the position of the two parties was this: Charles asked how he could raise an army for defence of the kingdom, if the powers enjoyed by his predecessors were stripped from him; and Parliament answered that it had no intention of allowing him any power whatever to raise such an army. (See the whole of the controversy in Rushworth).

The campaign in the north was speedily ended by the advance of the Scots, (August 2), and by the rout of the small English detachment that guarded the fords of the Tyne at Newburn. The Scots then occupied Newcastle, and England to all intent lay at their mercy. Nothing could have better suited the opponents of the king. A treaty was patched up at Ripon which amounted virtually to an agreement to subsidise the Scotch army in the interest of the Parliament. The Scots consented to stay where they were in consideration of eight hundred and fifty pounds a day, failing the payment of which it was open to them to continue their march southward and impose their own terms. Charles could not possibly raise such a sum without recourse to Parliament, and the assembly with which he had now to do was that which is known to history as the Long Parliament.

Within seven months, (May 1641), it had passed an Act to prevent its dissolution without its own consent, and having thus secured itself, it allowed the English Army to be disbanded, while the Scots, having played their part, retired once more across the Tweed. It would be tedious to follow the widening of the breach during the year 1641. Both parties saw that war was inevitable, and both struggled hard to keep the militia each in its own hands. The scramble was supremely ridiculous, since it was all for a prize not worth the snatching. Charles has been censured for throwing the whole military organisation out of gear because he wished to employ it for other objects than the safety of the kingdom, but it would be difficult, I think, for any one to explain what military organisation existed.

By the showing of the Parliamentary lawyers themselves, there was no statute to regulate it except the Statute of Winchester; in strictness there was no legal requirement for men to equip themselves otherwise than as in the year 1285. It was to the party that first made an army, not to that which preferred the sounder claim to regulate the militia, that victory was to belong. Strafford had perceived this long before, but three years were yet to pass before Parliament should realise it. The few movements worth noting in the scramble may be very briefly summarised. The king reluctantly consented to transfer the power of impressment to the justices of the peace with approval of Parliament, and abandoned his right to compel men to service outside their counties. But he refused to concede to Parliament the nomination of lord-lieutenants or the custody of strong places, and Parliament therefore simply arrogated to itself these privileges without further question. In July, 1642, the Commons resolved to levy an army of ten thousand men, in August the King unfurled the Royal Standard at Nottingham; and so the English Civil War began.

The war would bring forth the Parliamentarian 'New Model Army' a superb organisation which would in turn evolve into the first true regiments of the crown under the Restoration of Charles II.

LEONAUR

ALSO FROM LEONAUR
AVAILABLE IN SOFTCOVER OR HARDCOVER WITH DUST JACKET

THE FALL OF THE MOGHUL EMPIRE OF HINDUSTAN *by H. G. Keene*—By the beginning of the nineteenth century, as British and Indian armies under Lake and Wellesley dominated the scene, a little over half a century of conflict brought the Moghul Empire to its knees.

LADY SALE'S AFGHANISTAN *by Florentia Sale*—An Indomitable Victorian Lady's Account of the Retreat from Kabul During the First Afghan War.

THE CAMPAIGN OF MAGENTA AND SOLFERINO 1859 *by Harold Carmichael Wylly*—The Decisive Conflict for the Unification of Italy.

FRENCH'S CAVALRY CAMPAIGN *by J. G. Maydon*—A Special Correspondent's View of British Army Mounted Troops During the Boer War.

CAVALRY AT WATERLOO *by Sir Evelyn Wood*—British Mounted Troops During the Campaign of 1815.

THE SUBALTERN *by George Robert Gleig*—The Experiences of an Officer of the 85th Light Infantry During the Peninsular War.

NAPOLEON AT BAY, 1814 *by F. Loraine Petre*—The Campaigns to the Fall of the First Empire.

NAPOLEON AND THE CAMPAIGN OF 1806 *by Colonel Vachée*—The Napoleonic Method of Organisation and Command to the Battles of Jena & Auerstädt.

THE COMPLETE ADVENTURES IN THE CONNAUGHT RANGERS *by William Grattan*—The 88th Regiment during the Napoleonic Wars by a Serving Officer.

BUGLER AND OFFICER OF THE RIFLES *by William Green & Harry Smith*—With the 95th (Rifles) during the Peninsular & Waterloo Campaigns of the Napoleonic Wars.

NAPOLEONIC WAR STORIES *by Sir Arthur Quiller-Couch*—Tales of soldiers, spies, battles & sieges from the Peninsular & Waterloo campaigns.

CAPTAIN OF THE 95TH (RIFLES) *by Jonathan Leach*—An officer of Wellington's sharpshooters during the Peninsular, South of France and Waterloo campaigns of the Napoleonic wars.

RIFLEMAN COSTELLO *by Edward Costello*—The adventures of a soldier of the 95th (Rifles) in the Peninsular & Waterloo Campaigns of the Napoleonic wars.

LEONAUR

ALSO FROM LEONAUR
AVAILABLE IN SOFTCOVER OR HARDCOVER WITH DUST JACKET

OFFICERS & GENTLEMEN *by Peter Hawker & William Graham*—Two Accounts of British Officers During the Peninsula War: Officer of Light Dragoons by Peter Hawker & Campaign in Portugal and Spain by William Graham .

THE WALCHEREN EXPEDITION *by Anonymous*—The Experiences of a British Officer of the 81st Regt. During the Campaign in the Low Countries of 1809.

LADIES OF WATERLOO *by Charlotte A. Eaton, Magdalene de Lancey & Juana Smith*—The Experiences of Three Women During the Campaign of 1815: Waterloo Days by Charlotte A. Eaton, A Week at Waterloo by Magdalene de Lancey & Juana's Story by Juana Smith.

JOURNAL OF AN OFFICER IN THE KING'S GERMAN LEGION *by John Frederick Hering*—Recollections of Campaigning During the Napoleonic Wars.

JOURNAL OF AN ARMY SURGEON IN THE PENINSULAR WAR *by Charles Boutflower*—The Recollections of a British Army Medical Man on Campaign During the Napoleonic Wars.

ON CAMPAIGN WITH MOORE AND WELLINGTON *by Anthony Hamilton*—The Experiences of a Soldier of the 43rd Regiment During the Peninsular War.

THE ROAD TO AUSTERLITZ *by R. G. Burton*—Napoleon's Campaign of 1805.

SOLDIERS OF NAPOLEON *by A. J. Doisy De Villargennes & Arthur Chuquet*—The Experiences of the Men of the French First Empire: Under the Eagles by A. J. Doisy De Villargennes & Voices of 1812 by Arthur Chuquet .

INVASION OF FRANCE, 1814 *by F. W. O. Maycock*—The Final Battles of the Napoleonic First Empire.

LEIPZIG—A CONFLICT OF TITANS *by Frederic Shoberl*—A Personal Experience of the 'Battle of the Nations' During the Napoleonic Wars, October 14th-19th, 1813.

SLASHERS *by Charles Cadell*—The Campaigns of the 28th Regiment of Foot During the Napoleonic Wars by a Serving Officer.

BATTLE IMPERIAL *by Charles William Vane*—The Campaigns in Germany & France for the Defeat of Napoleon 1813-1814.

SWIFT & BOLD *by Gibbes Rigaud*—The 60th Rifles During the Peninsula War.

AVAILABLE ONLINE AT www.leonaur.com
AND FROM ALL GOOD BOOK STORES
07/09

LEONAUR

ALSO FROM LEONAUR
AVAILABLE IN SOFTCOVER OR HARDCOVER WITH DUST JACKET

AN APACHE CAMPAIGN IN THE SIERRA MADRE *by John G. Bourke*—An Account of the Expedition in Pursuit of the Chiricahua Apaches in Arizona, 1883.

BILLY DIXON & ADOBE WALLS *by Billy Dixon and Edward Campbell Little*—Scout, Plainsman & Buffalo Hunter, *Life and Adventures of "Billy" Dixon* by Billy Dixon and *The Battle of Adobe Walls* by Edward Campbell Little (*Pearson's Magazine*).

WITH THE CALIFORNIA COLUMN *by George H. Petis*—Against Confederates and Hostile Indians During the American Civil War on the South Western Frontier, *The California Column, Frontier Service During the Rebellion* and *Kit Carson's Fight With the Comanche and Kiowa Indians.*

THRILLING DAYS IN ARMY LIFE *by George Alexander Forsyth*—Experiences of the Beecher's Island Battle 1868, the Apache Campaign of 1882, and the American Civil War.

INDIAN FIGHTS AND FIGHTERS *by Cyrus Townsend Brady*—Indian Fights and Fighters of the American Western Frontier of the 19th Century.

THE NEZ PERCÉ CAMPAIGN, 1877 *by G. O. Shields & Edmond Stephen Meany*—Two Accounts of Chief Joseph and the Defeat of the Nez Percé, *The Battle of Big Hole* by G. O. Shields and *Chief Joseph, the Nez Percé* by Edmond Stephen Meany.

CAPTAIN JEFF OF THE TEXAS RANGERS *by W. J. Maltby*—Fighting Comanche & Kiowa Indians on the South Western Frontier 1863-1874.

SHERIDAN'S TROOPERS ON THE BORDERS *by De Benneville Randolph Keim*—The Winter Campaign of the U. S. Army Against the Indian Tribes of the Southern Plains, 1868-9.

GERONIMO *by Geronimo*—The Life of the Famous Apache Warrior in His Own Words.

WILD LIFE IN THE FAR WEST *by James Hobbs*—The Adventures of a Hunter, Trapper, Guide, Prospector and Soldier.

THE OLD SANTA FE TRAIL *by Henry Inman*—The Story of a Great Highway.

LIFE IN THE FAR WEST *by George F. Ruxton*—The Experiences of a British Officer in America and Mexico During the 1840's.

ADVENTURES IN MEXICO AND THE ROCKY MOUNTAINS *by George F. Ruxton*—Experiences of Mexico and the South West During the 1840's.

AVAILABLE ONLINE AT www.leonaur.com
AND FROM ALL GOOD BOOK STORES
07/09

www.ingramcontent.com/pod-product-compliance
Lightning Source LLC
Chambersburg PA
CBHW021059090426
42738CB00006B/413